Behind

the

BOTTOM LINE

Behind

the

BOTTOM LINE

POWERING

BUSINESS LIFE

with SPIRITUAL WISDOM

Stephen R. Graves and Thomas G. Addington

JOSSEY-BASS
A Wiley Imprint
www.josseybass.com

Published by Jossey-Bass
A Wiley Imprint
989 Market Street, San Francisco, CA 94103-1741   www.josseybass.com

Jossey-Bass books and products are available through most bookstores. To contact
Jossey-Bass directly call our Customer Care Department within the U.S. at
800-956-7739, outside the U.S. at 317-572-3986, or fax 317-572-4002.

Jossey-Bass also publishes its books in a variety of electronic formats. Some content
that appears in print may not be available in electronic books.

Unless otherwise noted in the text, scripture quotations are from The HOLY BIBLE:
New International Version, copyright © 1973, 1978, 1984. Used by permission of
Zondervan Bible Publishers.

Library of Congress Cataloging-in-Publication Data

Graves, Stephen R., date.
   Behind the bottom line: powering business life with spiritual wisdom
/ Stephen R. Graves and Thomas G. Addington.—1st ed.
      p. cm.
Includes bibliographical references and index.
      ISBN 0-7879-6467-0 (alk. paper)
   1. Businesspeople—Religious life. 2. Business—Religious
aspects—Christianity. I. Addington, Thomas G., date. II. Title.
   BV4596.B8 G73 2002
   248.8'8—dc21

                                                              2002014345

Printed in the United States of America

FIRST EDITION
HB Printing   10 9 8 7 6 5 4 3 2 1

Contents

Acknowledgments

Few writing projects have been more fun and challenging at the same time as has this book. Why, you might ask? Because it has long been a passion of ours to blend the common best practices of today's business world with the magnificent reservoir of the Scriptures, which is not always easy, but always beneficial. In this book we do just that.

Thanks to Steve Caldwell, Lois Flowers, and Kristie Reimer for helping us shape the words in their original form as articles.

Thanks to Bob Tamasy, who helped us compile, edit, and reshape much of the material into book form.

Thanks to Chip MacGregor, our agent, good friend, and a guy who kind of grows on you.

Thanks to Sheryl Fullerton and the rest of the Jossey-Bass team. We are pleased to be partnering with you guys.

This book is dedicated to the men and women in vocational ministry who have the passion and burden to be relevant in today's marketplace, and to the men and women of faith in the business community who are daily integrating the Grand Book of God into their own work settings. We give you all a standing ovation.

Introduction

Have you ever been to a live stage play? Perhaps you have enjoyed a sophisticated Broadway show, a presentation by a local theater troupe, or a musical produced by students at the high school in your area. Whatever your experience has been, think for a moment: As you were watching the play, how much time did you spend wondering about what was happening out of sight, behind the stage?

Over the years, we have enjoyed taking in outstanding theater productions during our business travels, including such captivating musicals as *The Lion King, Les Miserables,* and *The Phantom of the Opera* in revered theaters in London. Each time, we have marveled at the artistry and professionalism of the performances, the actors and singers demonstrating their exquisite training and preparation. The stage sets were breathtaking. Everything moved seamlessly from scene to scene, with everything in its place, working in concert to achieve the desired tone and to convey a specific message.

On several occasions, however, we have had the opportunity to observe plays from the other side—from behind the scenes. What we've seen from there was in striking contrast with what the audience was watching. Behind the curtains and the theatrical backdrops was a frenetic collage of seemingly random activity, with nothing looking coordinated. Performers wandered about from place to place, appearing to be totally disconnected from the panorama transpiring on stage. Stagehands stood nearby, conversing and casually awaiting the moment for the next set change. Stage props and equipment were piled and scattered everywhere in no apparent order, looking almost as if they had been carelessly cast aside. Unlike the theatrical magic occurring just a few feet away, backstage, there was no pretense of beauty or any concern about aesthetics.

Interestingly, the seeming chaos behind the scenes was somehow transformed into a wonderfully coherent and cohesive presentation on stage. The audience thoroughly enjoyed the performance without any notion of the unseen efforts required to make it a success—and that is as it should be.

We have found a similar experience in speaking at various business and men's conferences around the country, such as at one of Wal-Mart's annual corporate events or at a large Promise Keepers gathering. The smooth, well-conceived program that unfolds at and around the podium bears little resemblance to the furious activity going on behind the scenes as speakers are prepped to take their turns, technicians scramble to make sure the high-tech sound and graphic pieces are ready to fall into place, and the platform manager desperately watches the clock to make certain everyone stays true to schedule, down to the minute.

In this book, *Behind the Bottom Line: Powering Business Life with Spiritual Wisdom,* it's our contention that in a like manner, the visible and tangible elements of a company's profit and loss statement are tremendously affected by many unseen but essential factors that cannot be measured in terms of dollars and cents—factors such as company culture, momentum, timing, opportunity, and leadership. How people think and act behind the curtain of the drama we call business life can influence the real bottom line for any business.

Behind-the-scenes happenings at a Broadway play are not made for show, but they *make* the show. Similarly, a quick glance through our table of contents reveals factors that function outside the realm of the traditional bottom line but have a profound influence on what will appear in the annual report: power, change, wealth, ambition, ethics, balance, stewardship, partnering, calling, rest, strategy, innovation, entrepreneurship, marketplace grace, and legacy. None of these will ever be included as a line item on any company's P&L statement, but the impact they have on the items that do show up there is immeasurable.

One reason for the intangible, unquantifiable quality of each of our chapter topics is that they each involve a spiritual dimension. Decades ago, spirituality and business were regarded as being as separate from each other as church and state, but in recent years, business publications, ranging from the *Wall Street Journal* to *Fortune* to the *Harvard Business Review,* have increasingly—and consistently—acknowledged the reality that spirituality is an intrinsic part of business and professional life. Today, people are desperately searching for something to power their lives, and it is our belief that this "battery pack" has to have a spiritual foundation.

Without question, spirituality can take on any number of forms in today's business environment, but through study—and personal experience—we have determined that the Bible is far and away the greatest resource for putting business life and spiritual wisdom together. In seminaries, scholars use theology as a means of organizing their explorations of the Scriptures. They employ biblical theology, systematic theology, historical theology, and relational theology in their quest to understand God and ultimate truth. However, in *Behind the Bottom Line,* we propose a fifth approach—*commerce theology*—as a human-made template by which we can organize biblical thinking as it relates to the business and professional world. We need a new way to look at God's truth with an eye to the marketplace of the twenty-first century.

The topics we have included in this book are neither exclusive nor exhaustive. No doubt, we could have addressed many other business-related issues beyond the fifteen we have included. But these fifteen issues reflect some of our thinking since we founded the *Life@Work* journal in 1997. As we published each edition of the magazine, we believed that the topics therein were highly relevant, and responses from our readers have confirmed our assumptions.

At the same time, we are not attempting to provide exhaustive discussion of any single topic. On some of them, entire volumes have been written, so it would be foolish for us to think that we were offering the final word on any. Our desire is simply to introduce you to the idea of commerce theology and to encourage you to consider each topic within the context of both biblical teaching and your own experience. For instance, have you ever paused to think about what God's perspective is on the challenges of confronting change in the business world or about what guidelines the Scriptures can provide for someone engaged in entrepreneurship?

We debated as to whether we should cluster topics that are related, but, ultimately, we chose instead to list them individually, linking them as fifteen pearls in a very valuable necklace of wisdom for today's workplace. Think of each topic as a vignette—a single glance to stimulate your thinking. To enhance this process, in each chapter we offer a biblical example—a character, an applicable text, or a parable—that serves as a snapshot of what God has to say about that particular topic. To some, this may seem a little too Bible-heavy, or too business-light. But our primary goal is to introduce you to the concept of tackling a relevant business issue through the lens of scripture.

And beyond that, we want to help you extend your own thinking beyond the ideas we present. For that reason, we close each chapter with a series of questions that can be used for self-evaluation or as a framework for a small group discussion. We also offer a suggested prayer, although the prayer is there merely to help you express your own thoughts and concerns to God. And, finally, we present a list of supplemental resources—books, articles, and tapes—that might be useful as you seek to dig more deeply into each topic and see how it applies to your own circumstances.

Some of the topics that follow may seem irrelevant to where you are in life at the moment, but we have found that in the course of a business day, a season of work, or an entire career, each issue will confront us in one way or another. We hope that our discussions will give you something to draw on during the inevitable difficult times ahead.

In a stage play, all that goes on behind the scenes may seem helter-skelter, but there is a clearly conceived plan for the use of each person, prop, and piece of equipment. The secret lies in the play's preparation—planning for how and when each element will be used over the course of the entire play rather than just dealing with one act at a time.

In the same way, the time to consider how to most effectively deal with achieving balance in our lives, how to build and maintain worthwhile relationships, and how to develop successful strategies for business should not be at the time a crisis arises. To handle issues appropriately and in ways that we won't regret requires thoughtful preparation, well in advance.

If you desire people to see a sense of order and purpose in your life, whether it's in your workplace, in your family, or in your avocational pursuits, you should ensure that there is a well-conceived plan of action for preventing crises from developing or for dealing with those that do come about. It is our hope that *Behind the Bottom Line: Powering Business Life with Spiritual Wisdom* will help you achieve this goal.

Behind
the
BOTTOM LINE

Power and the Reactor Factor

A s president of his company, one of the best things Henry did was, well, act presidential. He knew that as soon as he returned to the office from a business trip, his employees would all jump to attention. He knew that whenever he summoned employees to his office, they would drop whatever they were doing and come running. And Henry knew that whenever he and his staff members were at odds over an issue, they would yield to his position. "Submit to those in authority," he knew the Bible stated, and people at his company had learned well the art of submitting.

What he didn't know was how anxiously his employees would count down the days until his next business trip. They dreaded seeing his car pull into the company parking lot, knowing that "Mr. Bivens" would, within minutes, turn their calm, peaceful environment into chaos as he barked one order after another. "It's like a dark cloud settles over our building when he arrives," one woman commented, and others readily agreed. Whenever Henry departed, it seemed that the "dark cloud" would leave with him.

Eventually, his domineering style began to take its toll. One employee would resign and then, as if the floodgates had been opened, several others would follow. But when his COO and his CFO turned in their resignations within a week of one another, Henry finally realized that there was a problem. These were key people who had always "watched his back," resolving difficult issues without complaining about the fact that he didn't care to deal with these issues and graciously handling his "emergencies," which should have been problems anticipated well in advance.

It was only then that the company's board of directors stepped in, prompted by the sudden turn of events to take an in-depth look at the company's health. When they hired a consultant to conduct a 360-degree review, the findings were startling. The impression of "all for one and one for all" that they had initially been given about the company's working environment became an impression of "all for one." They knew that for the future of the corporation, some drastic measures would be required.

■ ■

Driving across western Arkansas on Interstate 40, motorists can't help but notice a mammoth concrete smokestack rising from the landscape. What appears to be smoke, however, is actually vapor. And it's coming not from a smokestack but from a cooling tower for one of the two reactors at Arkansas Nuclear One (ANO).

Like the one hundred-plus other nuclear reactors around the country, the units at Arkansas Nuclear One in Russellville, Arkansas, were designed and constructed with safety in mind. The reactors are operated by highly qualified technicians who are trained, tested, and retrained in certified programs. And they are constantly monitored by on-site inspectors from the U.S. Nuclear Regulatory Commission. As a result, these two reactors produce nearly 28 percent of the electricity consumed in Arkansas, in a manner that is both clean and safe—for the people who live in the surrounding area *and* for the environment.

The smooth operation of ANO stands in stark contrast with the disaster that occurred in April 1986 at the Chernobyl nuclear power plant in Ukraine (part of the former Soviet Union). That horrific event—by far the most severe accident ever to occur at a commercial nuclear power facility—is believed to have resulted from a severely flawed reactor design and serious mistakes made by plant operators. The accident destroyed the reactor, killed thirty-one people (one person immediately and the rest within three months), and contaminated large areas of Belarus, Ukraine, and Russia, according to information on the Nuclear Energy Institute's Web site.

These are two different power plants, with two vastly different scenarios. At ANO, power effectively harnessed provides much-needed electricity for thousands of homes and businesses. At Chernobyl, power dangerously out of control put into motion a series of unstoppable events that allowed a significant amount of radioactive material to escape into the environment, forever altering the landscape and the lives of hundreds of thousands of people.

What these two sites had in common was the use of nuclear energy to produce electricity. Where they differed was in their handling of that energy, which made all the difference in how each would be fulfilling its mission. The Chernobyl plant failed miserably, and it was destroyed in the process, whereas the ANO plant has been a good steward of the power entrusted to it, and it remains productive and safe.

Most people never step inside a nuclear power plant, much less go near any kind of radioactive material. But whether we realize it or not, most of us have been given a certain amount of power. And we are all responsible for the way we handle that power, whether it places us over a hundred thousand employees at an international corporation or puts us in charge of two small children in our home.

Not everyone deals with power the same way, of course. The philosopher Aristotle believed that every virtue consists of the mean that lies between two extremes: excess and deficiency. For example, the virtue of generosity lies between waste (excess) and stinginess (deficiency). Likewise, power under control lies between the two extremes of power abuse (excess) and power neglect (deficiency).

It's not difficult to think of power abusers; Adolf Hitler, Jim Jones, and Slobodan Milosevic readily come to mind. And we all know people who are guilty of power neglect. There's the highly skilled graphic artist who panders his time away loading boxes at the warehouse because he won't take the initiative to get a job where he can use his gifts. Or there's the executive in the family business who was promoted because he's related to the owner but who has no desire to acquire the competencies he needs to be a capable leader. And then there is the husband who is so wrapped up in his work that he frequently fails to come home for dinner, read to his children, or spend time with his wife.

And then there are those who have found that sweet spot between the two extremes. There's the politician who realizes that power, at times, can be fleeting. There's the CEO who understands that with authority comes responsibility. There's the police officer, the cardiovascular surgeon, the high school principal, and the journalist who recognize that to be effective, they should neither abuse nor abdicate their power.

There are many manifestations of power in the Scriptures: the creative power God used to bring the universe into existence, the military power displayed by the armies of Israel as they conquered the Promised Land, the economic power of Solomon's kingdom, the supernatural power demonstrated by the miracles of Jesus—in His resurrection and in the coming of the Holy Spirit, and so on. The list of powerful people is just as compelling: Abraham, Joseph, Moses, David, Daniel, Esther, Nebuchadnezzar, Pilate, Agrippa, and the Apostle Paul, to name just a sampling. Some of these people recognized that their authority came from God; others did not. Some abused their power, some used it effectively, some abdicated it—and some, over the course of their lives, did all three.

Moses, the great lawgiver, falls into the latter category. For the most part, however, he got it right. He discovered Aristotle's mean—the perfect balance in knowing when to exercise his power and when to keep it under wraps—and he handled it with grace, compassion, and wisdom.

A PORTRAIT *of* POWER

Acts 7:22 says that Moses was "educated in all the wisdom of the Egyptians and was powerful in speech and action." A brief review of a few of his accomplishments verifies that description. After standing his ground during numerous confrontations with Pharaoh and coordinating the exodus of two million Israelites from Egypt, he led that same group of complainers around an inhospitable desert for forty years.

Think about it. Moses was responsible for some six hundred thousand men, their wives, their children, their personal belongings, and their livestock. That amounts to about two million people and who knows how many cows, sheep, and goats. He not only had to provide food and water for all these people and creatures in a hostile environment where there was neither, but he also was responsible for resolving all their disputes and maintaining peace in the camp. He had help with that, of course, but ultimately he was in charge.

We marvel when someone turns a failing company around in a year, wins a big military battle after several weeks, or achieves a great victory in court after a three-month trial. But as significant as those accomplishments are, they pale in comparison with the work of Moses. He didn't just guide the Israelites for a few weeks, a few months, or a few years, he led them for *four decades.*

Moses was to the children of Israel what Warren Buffett has been to Berkshire Hathaway, what Jack Welch was to General Electric, and what Sam Walton was to Wal-Mart. There is a difference, however. Buffett has led Berkshire Hathaway for only slightly more than three decades, Walton was at the helm of his company for about the same length of time, and Welch led GE for just over twenty years.

Keeping the same leadership post for forty years is a tall order under any circumstances. But the people Moses led didn't even want to be there! They complained incessantly about how much better off they had been as slaves in Egypt. They grumbled about the food that God provided for them. And they even occasionally rebelled against Moses'—and God's—authority over them.

But despite all the pains his power brought him, Moses neither threw in the towel nor evolved into a tyrannical dictator. He persevered, strengthened by his relationship with the God he had come to know "face to face" (Deuteronomy 34:10).

Moses wasn't perfect, of course. Scripture records at least two occasions when God got angry with him, and both times had to do with Moses' response to the power he had been given.

In the first case, he tried to abdicate it. When God called Moses to deliver His people from bondage in Egypt, Moses had been working as a shepherd for forty years. So when God gave Moses his assignment at the burning bush, it's no wonder that he had misgivings. He fired off one objection after another: "I'm not qualified." "What if the people don't believe me?" "I've never been good at speaking in public." "Send someone else to do it." (See Exodus 4:1–13.)

That final comment was the last straw. However, although Exodus 4:14 states that the Lord's "anger burned against Moses," in His compassion, He selected Aaron, Moses' older brother, to serve as Moses' spokesman. God didn't allow Moses to neglect the power he had been given, but He did give him a partner in leadership.

Moses also triggered God's anger by abusing his power. It was another occasion when the people were complaining because they had no water to drink. But rather than maintain his composure as he had done many other times, Moses lost his temper. God had instructed him and Aaron to gather the people together, to speak to a rock in their presence, and then to allow them to drink the water that came from the rock.

Instead, Moses struck the rock twice with his staff. Water gushed out, but the outburst caused Moses and Aaron to forfeit the privilege of entering the Promised Land. "Because you did not trust in me enough to honor me as holy in the sight of the Israelites," God told them, "you will not bring this community into the land I give them" (Numbers 20:12).

Moses' reaction to his punishment is telling. He was deeply grieved that he would not be able to enter the Promised Land. But rather than sulk or pitch a fit about the unfairness of it all, Moses resumed the march toward Canaan. The secret to his response—and, in turn, to his ability to maintain a godly approach to power—lies in a particular character trait that is not commonly associated with powerful people.

Numbers 12:3 (KJV) says that Moses was "very meek, above all the men which were upon the face of the earth." The word *meek* often brings to mind the picture of a timid, feeble person who is afraid to stand up for himself. For Moses, however, nothing could be further from the truth.

Meekness does have an element of gentleness associated with it, but behind that gentleness is the strength of steel. Think of a once-wild horse that has been trained to submit to a bit and a bridle. "It is not a spineless gentleness, a sentimental fondness, a passive quietism," writes William Barclay in *New Testament Words* (The Westminster Press, 1964). "It is a strength under control."

POSITIONAL *Versus* PERSONAL POWER

The meekness that Moses demonstrated was an integral part of his *personal* power, whereas his specific role as leader of Israel was an example of the *positional* power that God had given him. Generally speaking, it is into those two categories that power—particularly as evidenced in the business world—falls.

Positional power is the ability to act based on one's station or platform in life. In the corporate world, a person's positional power is measured by his title, the size and placement of his office, his salary, the number of stock options he has, the number of employees he has under his control, and whether he drives his own car or has a limousine at his beck and call.

The very nature of these trappings reveals that positional power is external, and, as such, it can come and go. When the president's term is over, he gives up the privilege of traveling in Air Force One. When a corporate CEO retires, he relinquishes his right to the corner office. On the flip side, when a thirty-year-old doctor completes a cardiac surgery residency and joins the surgical team at a large hospital, she suddenly has a great deal of positional power that she never had as a medical student. When a twenty-six-year-old accountant earns an M.B.A. from Harvard Business School, his earning potential rises dramatically, simply because he now holds an advanced degree from a prestigious university. Inside, the doctor and the accountant are still the same people they've always been, but, outwardly, they wield much more influence than they did before.

Personal power, on the other hand, is based on moral authority. It represents a source of energy that flows from the inside out. From a theological perspective, a person with this type of power knows who he is. He knows what his skills are. He knows what he was created to do. He has an eternal sense of purpose and, as a result, his life is characterized by peace, contentment, and integrity.

Personal power is tied to reputation, which means that if a person loses his reputation, he also can lose his personal power. But in today's rapidly changing marketplace, the loss of positional power is far more common.

By defining power this way, we don't mean to reinforce the misconception that personal power is good and that positional power is bad. Going back to Aristotle's balance between two extremes, both types of power can be either abused or neglected, and both kinds can be used properly. The Bible tells of many people who failed to exercise their positional power correctly, but it also is full of examples of people who used both personal and positional power to accomplish great things.

Moses, for example, never would have been able to lead the Israelites for forty years without a good deal of personal and positional power. True, the people were often rebellious and ornery. But if they had not recognized that Moses' power was based on the ultimate moral authority and that his position was God-given, they would have hightailed it back to Egypt before the first batch of manna ever appeared on the ground.

Moses certainly had neither personal power nor positional power when, as an infant, his mother placed him among the reeds of the Nile. When Pharaoh's daughter found him and adopted him as her own son, his positional power shot up exponentially. He was now a member of the king's court, and he had access to all the privileges that accompanied such a distinction.

Scripture says nothing to make us think that Moses didn't also have some degree of personal power in that setting. But we do know that when he killed an Egyptian who was beating a Hebrew slave, his own people rejected him—a clear indication that whatever personal power he had wasn't enough to impress the Israelites, at least not at that time in his life (Exodus 2:11–14).

The first forty years of Moses' life ended with his running away to Midian to escape prosecution for the murder of the Egyptian. The next forty years served as a time of character development for Israel's future leader. As a shepherd, the only positional power he exerted was over the sheep. And his personal power was limited to the influence he may have exerted as a husband and father.

The burning bush experience changed all that. Moses' life-changing encounter with God gave him all the personal and positional power he needed to accomplish a seemingly impossible task. Not that anyone else could tell the difference right away. Compared with Pharaoh, Moses appeared as powerful as an ant about to get crushed by an elephant. Pharaoh had a mighty army at his disposal. He had the best magicians that Egypt could offer at his service. And he had all the clout and glory that went along with being the king of the most powerful country on earth.

Given those odds, Moses didn't stand a chance. But he had one thing that Pharaoh didn't have: a personal relationship with the all-powerful God of Abraham, Isaac, and Jacob. That relationship—and the power it held—was what sustained him as he warned Pharaoh about the plagues, as he led the Israelites across the Red Sea (Exodus 14), as he guided them to victory over the Amalekites (Exodus 17:8–16), as he received God's law on Mount Sinai (Exodus 20), as he dealt with the disobedience and constant complaints of the people, and as he led them in the wilderness for forty years.

Moses *on* Power

As those final forty years drew to a close, perhaps Moses did some deep thinking about his life, his career, his beloved Israelites, and his relationship with the great "I Am." As he stood at the top of Mount Nebo and gazed over the Promised Land, he likely felt the familiar pangs of sadness about the sin that ultimately kept him from entering the land with his people. If, at that moment, Moses had been asked to give a brief summary of his life learnings about power, he might have touched on the following themes:

1. POWER IS A SACRED TRUST.

   It doesn't matter if we inherit our power, if we attain it gradually as we rise through the corporate ranks, or if we receive it by virtue of being elected to a specific post. Whatever the case, it doesn't really belong to us, and we have no guarantees that it will last. The only thing we know for sure is that, for as long as we have it, we are responsible for using it wisely.

   When God gives us a certain amount of power, He expects us to be good stewards of it. Power is never an end in itself. Like money, it's a tool—to influence someone, to help a cause, to right a wrong, to create an opportunity. It's up to us to figure out why we have been blessed with our power and then to make sure we use it correctly.

2. OUR CHARACTER IS TESTED BY HOW WE USE OUR GOD-GIVEN POWER.

   There's nothing like a big dose of power to find out what someone is really made of. If a person whose life is marked by self-control, honesty, and integrity receives a big promotion or is appointed to a top position, his whole approach to his newfound power will be quite different from that of someone who is devoid of character. But that doesn't mean that the first guy won't struggle with handling power correctly.

   "Power is as dangerous as unstable dynamite, not only to those it is used on but [also] to those who exercise it," writes Tom Marshall in *Understanding Leadership* (Sovereign Word Ltd., 1991). "Lord Acton, the British statesman, is remembered for his famous dictum, 'All power corrupts, and absolute power corrupts absolutely.' History is littered with the sad evidence that proves the correctness of his judgment, the wreckage of good men and good women who began with the best of intentions but were corrupted and destroyed by the power they wielded."

3.   POSITIONAL POWER AND PERSONAL POWER MUST NEVER BE
     CONFUSED.

If a significant part of our authority stems from our position—as a CEO, a business owner, a college president, or an elected official, there's always a danger that we might slip into the mode of assuming that people do what we say because of our own personal influence over them. Then, when that authority slips away—when a new guy takes office or we're replaced by a new CEO, we lose our identity. That's why it's important to remember that positional power can come and go, but personal power often grows over time.

4.   THE MORE POWER WE GIVE AWAY, THE MORE POWERFUL WE
     BECOME.

This story is a familiar one. Moses' father-in-law, Jethro, came to visit his family in the Israelite camp. The next day, Moses opened court and began mediating the people's disputes, from morning until evening. When Jethro realized that this was Moses' daily practice, he gave him some advice that has stood the test of time, particularly in organizational management circles. Jethro told Moses,

> What you are doing is not good. You and these people who come to you will only wear yourselves out. The work is too heavy for you; you cannot handle it alone. . . . You must be the people's representative before God and bring their disputes to Him. Teach them the decrees and laws, and show them the way to live and the duties they are to perform. But select capable men from all the people—men who fear God, trustworthy men who hate dishonest gain—and appoint them as officials over thousands, hundreds, fifties, and tens. . . . That will make your load lighter, because they will share it with you (Exodus 18:17–22).

Moses took his father-in-law's advice. He didn't figure it out on his own, but once he was shown the value of empowering the people, he didn't try to hoard all the power. For Moses, giving power away not only was efficient and effective, but it also significantly expanded the depth of his leadership. That, in turn, helped him in the continual exercise of power that was required as he led the Israelites.

5. WHEN GOD GIVES US POWER, IT IS UP TO HIM TO KEEP US IN
    POWER.

Throughout the course of his leadership tenure, Moses had significant challenges to his power. But whether they came from members of his inner circle (Miriam and Aaron) or from rebels among the people (see Numbers 16), he never fought back. He left vindication up to God, and God never failed him.

If we're in a position of leadership, it's not a matter of *whether* people will challenge our power, it's a matter of *when*. At that point, we are faced with the same three choices we face as we deal with any other aspect of power. We can overreact, we can unplug, or we can balance on that sweet spot in the middle and wait for God to act on our behalf. "It will require discipline to take the journey and to live with the mockery, the condescending comments, the inevitable second-guessing," Charles Swindoll writes in *Moses: A Man of Selfless Dedication* (Word Publishing, 1999). "You must have the kind of discipline it takes to say, 'Lord God, you are the one who set me on this course, and until you say otherwise, this is the direction I'm going to walk. My critics are getting louder and more in number and closer. Silence them. Or at least, stop my ears.'"

6. THE MORE POWER WE HAVE, THE MORE FAITH WE NEED.

The book of Deuteronomy closes with the following words: "Since then [Moses' death], no prophet has risen in Israel like Moses, whom the Lord knew face to face, who did all those miraculous signs and wonders the Lord sent him to do in Egypt—to Pharaoh and to all his officials and to his whole land. For no one has ever shown the mighty power or performed the awesome deeds that Moses did in the sight of all Israel" (Deuteronomy 34:10–12).

What a fitting epitaph for one of the greatest leaders of all time. But it never would have been written had Moses not been a man of growing faith. He led the people one step at a time. He never knew how God was going to accomplish His promises; he simply believed that He would, in fact, accomplish them. Initially, Moses didn't really want any power—or any of the frustrations and responsibilities that came with it. But as he watched God work, he began to trust Him more. And as he came to trust Him more, he learned to bring each struggle, each pain, each frustration, and each temptation associated with his power to God.

His relationship with God was his sole means for dealing with his power. With that relationship, he was as effective as the smoothly operating nuclear power plant in Russellville, Arkansas. Without it, he would have self-destructed like the reactor at Chernobyl, leaving the Israelites to suffer from the fallout caused by a leader who couldn't handle his power.

Therein lies the most important lesson of all: Seek God, not power. Doing the opposite only leads to disaster.

Evaluating Power

Power is something we all have, to one degree or another. Some, because of their positions or personalities, seem to have more power at their disposal. But we all have some measure of power within our spheres of influence. The question is, how will that power be used? Now would be a good time for you to evaluate your own use, misuse, or abuse of power. The following three questions are designed to help you arrive at an honest self-appraisal and, if necessary, consider steps to enable you to more appropriately direct your power to the benefit of everyone involved.

1. In what ways might you currently be abusing the power available to you?

    Consider your relationships with those you report to, your peers, and those who report to you. Do you influence others through mutual respect and concern, or have you learned ways to achieve your purposes, regardless of what others think? Discuss this with someone you can be honest with, and be willing to receive honest and insightful feedback.

2. Can you think of any times that you have neglected your personal power?

    Have you ever failed to pursue ways to fully maximize your gifts, talents, and skills? Perhaps you're failing to do this right now. Or maybe you have become so wrapped up in your career that you have forgotten to give a high priority to other areas of your life in which your power is needed, such as your family, your church, or your community. Candidly appraising yourself in this area may be difficult; you may even say "ouch!" a time or two. But consider the alternative of ignoring this reality in your life.

3. WHAT STEPS SHOULD YOU TAKE TO FIND THE "SWEET SPOT BETWEEN THE TWO EXTREMES"—NOT ABUSING YOUR POWER, BUT ALSO NEGLECTING TO USE IT PRODUCTIVELY AND POSITIVELY?

It's not enough to admit your tendency to misuse power in your work and personal environment. If you typically use it in inappropriate ways, it's important to explore what changes you should make to align more consistently with the biblical perspective on power. Have a friend—or members of your small group—help you consider the problems and possible solutions.

PRAYING *About* POWER

Consider the following prayer as a guide to seeking God's help so that you can honestly reconsider your approach to using power at work, in your home, or anywhere else.

Lord, power can be a seductive tool, used in self-centered ways to manipulate others and accomplish one's own purposes. In the workplace, the result can be equivalent to what happened at Chernobyl. Power can be ignored and neglected to avoid unwanted confrontation, and, in commerce, power is more often abused or misused than used in ways that are true to Your Word. I want my power to benefit others as well as myself. Enable me to sincerely review what kind of power wielder I am and help me be willing to make necessary changes.

Recommended Resources on Power

Descending into Greatness, by Bill Hybels, Zondervan, 1994.
Empowerment Takes More Than a Minute, by Ken Blanchard, Berrett-Koehler, 1998.
Moses: A Man of Selfless Dedication, by Charles Swindoll, W Publishing Group, 1999.
A Tale of Three Kings, by Gene Edwards, Tyndale House, 1992.

CHAPTER 2

The Gospel of Change

Liz was frazzled. For ten years she had enjoyed working in the finance department of her company, but lately it seemed as if the "powers-that-be" were determined to make her life miserable.

Virtually every week, her superiors were calling staff meetings to inform the staff of changes that were going to be made—such as a new computer system, new software, or new weekly reports with tighter deadlines. And on top of that, there would be staff cutbacks, largely accomplished by early-outs and attrition. What's new? had suddenly become a question that Liz dreaded to hear.

"I'm as much a team player as anyone," she confided to a friend outside the company. "I do all I can to cooperate with and support my supervisors and coworkers. But lately it seems as if they keep changing the rules of the game, just for the sake of making changes. If it's not changing policies on how we handle financial records, it's some new technological gizmo they need for everybody to get up to speed on by yesterday. And if it's not that, then they come up with some crazy new company-wide policy—without asking for input from the people most affected. If this keeps up, I'll be lobbying for a change myself—a job with a new company!"

Yet after spending more than a decade with her company—most of which she had enjoyed—and developing very close friendships with several of her coworkers, change to a new company wasn't very inviting for Liz. She wasn't happy with how things had been going lately, but she felt that sometimes the known—no matter how unpleasant—was preferable to the unknown. So, after weeks of worrying, and occasionally grumbling out loud, Liz finally got around to what she knew she should have done in the first place: she prayed, asking God for wisdom in how to cope with the multitude of changes she was facing and for a sense of peace about whatever steps she needed to take.

■ ■

In 1999, Hewlett-Packard Company (HP) ushered in a new era of leadership when it appointed forty-four-year-old Carleton Fiorina as CEO. One of the world's top female executives, Fiorina, had managed the spin-off of Lucent Technologies from AT&T in 1996, and then she helped transform the slow-moving communications-equipment business into a major Internet player.

Fiorina was the first woman to lead a major computer company or a Dow 30 firm. According to *Business Week,* her hiring also marked the first time in HP's sixty-year history that the company reached beyond its employee base to fill a top job. But she wasn't recruited so that HP could reach a diversity goal; she was hired to lead change in a rapidly changing industry.

Fiorina's challenge was clear. With HP's quarterly earnings failing to meet Wall Street expectations and competitors like Sun Microsystems and IBM taking the lead in Internet commerce, HP was often seen as conservative, old-fashioned, and slow. Despite some recent improvements, fresh leadership was needed, and that's exactly what Fiorina planned to provide. "We're going to need to reinvigorate our sense of speed, our sense of urgency," she said the day she was hired. That speed and urgency was a factor in HP's pursuit of the $19.6 billion acquisition of Compaq Computer in 2002, which would vault the corporation to the forefront of the high-tech industry.

The Fiorina story is representative of cover articles seen regularly in business publications. One week it's "Fidelity: New President, New Strategy"; the next week it's "Can Rick Thomas Reinvent Xerox?" And although these headlines usually include the name of a top executive, they somehow manage to sound impersonal. Even layoff announcements are often dismissed as distant downsizing brought on by such ambiguous factors as production declines or competitive pressures.

But that casual detachment becomes intensely personal when the new CEO's revitalization strategy means that *we* have to alter the way we do our job, when *we* have a personality conflict with the boss who was hired to save our company, or when the pink slips appear on our desk. Fiorina told *Business Week* that she planned to use a scalpel rather than a machete as she made changes to propel HP into the Internet Age. Even so, the changes had a great impact on thousands of individuals in very personal ways.

So while publications like *The Wall Street Journal, Management Review,* and *Fortune* address some aspect of change in almost every issue, one fact remains: change is only a theory until it shows up at our front door. Until we actually lose our job, receive an unwanted overseas assignment, or learn that the company we work for has been sold, the concept of change remains just an academic idea discussed in some *Harvard Business Review* case study. But when it shows up at our desk, it does so as a deeply personal visitor calling us out in a transparent way by our first name, making us feel vulnerable.

In these initial years of the new millennium, the pace of change is constantly accelerating. Change in the future will be dramatic as the economy continues to embrace globalization and as the Internet continues to revolutionize the way business is conducted. As always, these changes won't just affect financial statements; they will affect the lives of individual people.

Of all the biblical events that illustrate the drama and dynamic of change, none has more significance than the birth of Jesus. In his beloved devotional book, *My Utmost for His Highest: 365 Daily Devotional* (1935), Oswald Chambers terms Him "the central point upon which all of time and eternity turn." Jesus arrived about two thousand years ago to redeem the world. That first Christmas marked the beginning of revolutionary changes—a transition from law to grace, from the Old Testament to the New Testament, from God's covenant with Israel to His covenant with the Church. Because Jesus came, we can have eternal life. But even more than that, the Scriptures teach that through the indwelling presence of Christ, believers can experience new life on earth before they depart for their heavenly home: "Therefore, if anyone is in Christ, he is a new creation; the old has gone, the new has come!" (2 Corinthians 5:17). That sounds like *real* change.

Indeed, Jesus brought—and continues to bring—change, both in the broad scheme of life and in the lives of individual men and women. For instance, in the biblical narrative, we see how His entry into the world had a deep and immediate personal impact on three characters: Mary, Joseph, and King Herod. Together, they offer compelling insight into how we can handle change in all areas of life. Every day is not a Christmas story, but every day is full of change. We are not Mary, Joseph, or Herod, but two thousand years have not altered the human responses to change.

ONE EVENT, THREE RESPONSES

Using the organizational change lingo, Mary might be labeled the "early adapter," Joseph the "hard sell," and Herod the "defiant resister."

Mary, in her early teens and engaged to an older teenager named Joseph, was the first to enter the picture. Imagine her surprise when the angel Gabriel arrived at her house with this message: "Greetings, you who are highly favored! The Lord is with you" (Luke 1:28). Mary was "greatly troubled at his words and wondered what kind of greeting this might be" (Luke 1:29). Imagine that the CEO of a large corporation shows up in the cubicle of a rank-and-file employee, sits down, and starts telling the employee what a great job he is doing for the company. Never having been visited by the CEO, the employee would probably sit on the other side of the desk and nervously wonder why the boss was *really* there.

The angel, however, quickly gave Mary the information she needed, telling her that she was going to give birth to the "Son of the Most High," who would "reign over the house of Jacob forever" (Luke 2:32, 33). After inquiring how this could happen to a virgin, Mary quickly accepted her new role, which was revealed by her response to the angel's words: "I am the Lord's servant. . . . May it be to me as you have said" (Luke 1:38). She was the model "early adapter."

Joseph's buy-in took a little longer. Upon learning that Mary was pregnant, and knowing that he wasn't the father, he planned to divorce her quietly so that she wouldn't be disgraced publicly. He apparently was thinking about how to handle the situation, when the angel of the Lord appeared to him in a dream and confirmed that the Holy Spirit had conceived Mary's baby. Once armed with the facts, Joseph embraced the change.

Herod, however, had a more optimistic public face than either Mary or Joseph but in reality was a defiant resister to the core. He only pretended to welcome change. When the Magi asked Herod where the king of the Jews was to be born, he put his research team to work. He questioned the chief priests and scribes about Jewish prophecy, and he secretly obtained additional information from the Magi about the exact time the star had appeared. Then he sent the Magi to Bethlehem with these instructions: "Go and make a careful search for the child. As soon as you find him, report to me, so that I too may go and worship him" (Matthew 2:8). Although his words indicated otherwise, Herod's only goal was to subvert and sabotage any change that this "one who has been born king of the Jews" might bring. To him, the birth of the Savior was a very real threat—one that had to be eliminated as soon as possible.

The responses of these three individuals are not unlike how people in organizations handle transitions and disruptions. Some jump on board eagerly and seem to lean into the change. Like Mary, they may not understand all the ramifications of the change, but they're willing to do whatever it takes to help it happen smoothly. Others, like Joseph, need time to get used to the idea of the change and require information to help them understand why the change is necessary. Once sold, they, too, become active participants. Others resist change at every turn. Wearing any number of different faces, they may appear to be in agreement, but behind the scenes, they minimize the need for the change and criticize those who drive it.

What does the Christmas story teach regarding change?

CHANGE POINTS

1. LIFE IS FULL OF THE UNEXPLAINABLE AND THE UNEXPECTED.

Mary and Joseph were living quietly when an angelic messenger with an incredible message transformed their existence. They weren't expecting this turn of events, and they didn't know how to explain it. The changes that happen to us today seldom have such a supernatural element attached to them, but they, too, often occur without warning.

One day it's business as usual. The next day, we lose our job—or we receive a large raise, our company is sold, or our spouse files for divorce.

Unexplainable and unexpected events are handed to people in different doses and at different times, but they're bound to happen sooner or later. Some things—like a big promotion—are welcome, but others are less desirable. The Apostle James writes, "Consider it pure joy, my brothers, whenever you face trials of many kinds, because you know that the testing of your faith develops perseverance" (James 1:1–2). Notice that James says "*whenever* you face trials of many kinds" (emphasis added). He uses the word *whenever* instead of *if* because he knows that times of difficulty will come for each of us. Trials and changes are unavoidable; the only thing we control is our response. God promises that if we maintain a joyful attitude (as Mary did), He will use the change to develop patience and perseverance in us.

2. PEOPLE NEED INFORMATION AND INSPIRATION DURING THE
    CHANGE PROCESS.

Unlike Mary, who received advance notice of what was to happen, Joseph didn't get any official information until he found out that his fiancée was pregnant. There was no time to get used to the idea; he woke up one day and his life was different. Fortunately, he didn't have to wait long for more data. The angel of the Lord soon appeared to him in a dream with a fact-filled message: "Joseph, son of David, do not be afraid to take Mary home as your wife, because what is conceived in her is from the Holy Spirit. She will give birth to a Son, and you are to give Him the name Jesus, because He will save His people from their sins (Matthew 1:20–21). In one dream, the angel told Joseph exactly what he needed to know, connecting the dots with at least five important pieces of information.

When facing a big change at work, we often need to know why it's happening and how it's going to affect us. We're quick to ask ourselves, "Will I have a new boss?" or "Will I have to share my cubicle with four other people?" or "Will I lose my company credit card?" Like Joseph, the more information we get, the easier it is to process the change. That's why it's so important for change leaders to keep their employees informed. As a general rule, the more we know, the more willingly we embrace the change.

The opposite is also true. Managers who initiate change often assume that both they and the people who will be affected by the change have the same facts, but that's often not true, according to John P. Kotter and Leonard A. Schlesinger. In a 1979 *Harvard Business Review* article on change strategies, they note that, "In either case, the difference in information that groups work with often leads to differences in analyses, which in turn can lead to resistance."

But we also need inspiration. This can't be conveyed in a memo that merely informs us of our new seating assignment; it must come from someone who personally assures us that everything is going to be okay. Mary and Joseph could draw from their knowledge of Jewish history to realize that they were about to participate in the fulfillment of biblical prophecy. But when the angel showed up, they needed someone to say, "Don't be afraid," which is what the angel did. Once they got over the shock of seeing the angel, they must have drawn incredible comfort from the fact that God cared enough to send an angel to explain what was about to happen. The role of a vision caster is crucial to a successful change process.

3.   It is normal to experience emotional turmoil during periods of change.

Matthew 1 and Luke 1 reveal that Mary was troubled when she found out about the coming birth of Christ and that in response to the news, Joseph was afraid and Herod was disturbed. In response to change, we are often troubled, scared, or disturbed. Ironically, the event that was about to take place in Bethlehem was a wonderful thing, but when Mary, Joseph, and Herod first learned of it, it looked less than desirable.

Imagine the emotional turmoil Mary and Joseph experienced. Though not yet married, they were legally bound together and could be separated only by divorce. A pregnancy at this point in their relationship would be scandalous. They knew the truth, but how did they explain it to their friends? It must have pained them to know that their reputations had been scarred by circumstances beyond their control.

"A change can make sense logically, but [it] can still lead to anxiety in the psychological dimension," writes Bob Biehl in *Thirty Days to Confident Leadership* (Broadman & Holman, 1998). Even the strongest followers of Christ experience emotional upheaval during periods of transition. That's because change often is accompanied by pain, and we hate to hurt. These feelings are legitimate, and they don't signify a lack of faith. In fact, feeling troubled about something actually can be good if it prompts us to pray.

4.   PEOPLE'S REACTIONS TO CHANGE REVEAL THEIR TRUE COLORS.

Matthew 1:19 reveals that Joseph was a "righteous man," which was why he didn't want to subject Mary to the disgrace of public divorce. The text also implies that he was thoughtful; he spent time "considering" what he should do (Matthew 1:20). Finally, the way Joseph behaved from the time he learned about Mary's pregnancy through the time the family returned from Egypt indicates that he was sensitive to supernatural leading. He wasn't bent on handling change his way; he was open to divine direction. All of these characteristics existed in Joseph's life before he was chosen to be Christ's earthly father.

Herod's true colors were also exposed. When the Magi arrived in Jerusalem, they probably had no idea what a chain reaction their inquiry would start. They merely wanted to pay homage to the Messiah. But their visit "produced on King Herod . . . a far different impression," writes Alfred Edersheim in *The Life and Times of Jesus the Messiah* (Eerdmans, 1976). "Unscrupulously cruel as Herod had always proved, even the slightest suspicion of danger to his rule—the bare possibility of the Advent of One, Who had such claims upon the allegiance of Israel, and Who, if acknowledged, would evoke the most intense movement on their part—must have struck terror in his heart."

When Herod found out that he had been outwitted by the Magi, he resorted to the only thing he knew—violence. When faced with a change that threatened his life, he fell apart because he had nothing to fall back on but his own deceptive nature. How strikingly this contrasts with Mary and Joseph, who, though concerned about their own well-being, trusted God and didn't try to take matters into their own hands.

JOINING GOD

Clearly, the preparation to handle change correctly doesn't begin when the change is initiated. We must be ready for change in order to respond well. From a spiritual standpoint, that preparation consists of several key ingredients.

During a transition, *we must not forget where we've been.* In the Old Testament, the children of Israel were constantly to remember change points of the past as a way to give them faith for change in the future. That's what the Passover celebration was all about—to help them remember how God miraculously delivered them from bondage in Egypt. Remembering how God has worked in the past remains a valuable tool for weathering change. We usually don't see it at the front end, but after we've survived a change, we can look back and review how God took care of us. Besides building faith, this gives us strength to face today's challenges.

When going through a change, *we can see only as far as our headlights illuminate.* Despite the uncertainty, we must look past the immediate changes to what God ultimately has in store. That's what Mary did. Still in the early days of her pregnancy, she had the foresight to say, "From now on, all generations will call me blessed, for the Mighty One has done great things for me" (Luke 1:48–49), while having little idea of what the next day might hold. According to Edersheim, each event connected with the birth of Christ came to Mary as a fresh discovery. "She knew the beginning, and she knew the end; but she knew not the path which led from the one to the other; and each step in it was a new revelation," he writes.

As followers of Christ who constantly experience change, it's also crucial for us to *maintain a relaxed view of God's sovereignty.* That may sound like a paradox, but it really is another way of looking at Romans 8:28: "And we know that in all things God works for the good of those who love Him, who have been called according to His purpose." Believers can depend on God to orchestrate events and circumstances according to His plan. With a relaxed view of God's sovereignty, we have a big view of God and a small view of ourselves. We are free to join what God has initiated; we don't have to make things happen that we hope God will join. Making something happen leads to high blood pressure, worry, and stress. Joining something that God is doing leads to peace, joy, and contentment. In the midst of change, followers of Christ can relax in the knowledge that they serve a God of purpose, order, and love who is willing and able to care for them.

Mary and Joseph had a relaxed view of God's sovereignty. What happened to them is something God planned from the foundation of the world; they simply were His agents in that plan. To think that they had something to do with dreaming up the immaculate conception would be ridiculous. It's no less ridiculous to initiate something—a new company, a new career, or a big project—on our own and then try to invite God to join in later. We're not supposed to be disinterested observers of our own lives, but we do need to recognize that God ultimately is in control, and, like Mary and Joseph, we're simply agents in His plan.

We Change; God Doesn't

A French author once said, "The only thing constant in life is change." That is particularly true for a believer; a life with Christ is a life of change. This presupposition is evident in the language used in scripture: change is inherent in such terms and phrases as *transformation, becoming new,* and *throwing off the old.* Change is also wrapped up in the whole concept of sanctification—the process in which we continually become more like Jesus over the course of our lives with Christ. If we are not experiencing change, we are not experiencing growth, and if we are not experiencing growth, we are not experiencing Christ.

Change is part of a life with Christ. It was true for Mary and Joseph, and it's true today for businesspeople who juggle family and church responsibilities while working in a fast-moving world of mergers, layoffs, globalization, and e-commerce. But this foundational principle is accompanied by an even more important fact—that the God we serve is a changeless God. Malachi 3:6a makes it clear: "I the Lord do not change."

This gives followers of Christ a solid foundation upon which to weather change. In the midst of our changing circumstances, God is both immutable and sovereign. "He is the rock that we can cling to when nothing else seems secure," writes Ed Young in *Against All Odds* (Nelson, 1992). "God is always working out His will, His plan, His purpose, His dreams in every realm of life. His plan for the destiny of mankind is being put forth in the everyday affairs of men, or otherwise this whole thing would be hopeless."

In *The Seven Habits of Highly Effective People* (Simon & Schuster, 1989), Stephen R. Covey observes that "people can't live with change if there's not a changeless core inside them." For the disciple of Christ, writes Young, "that changeless core is Jesus Christ living within us, our hope of glory." For the person who has not yet met Christ, however, that core is elusive; it cannot be obtained apart from a personal relationship with Jesus, the Messiah who was born two thousand years ago in Bethlehem and lives today in the hearts of those who love Him.

The Christmas story is for all of us. But it holds unique meaning for those of us who know Christ in a personal way. The baby born in a manger grew up to die on a cross for the sins of the world. He took the punishment for our sins, which gives each of us the opportunity to experience the change of a lifetime by receiving Him as Lord and Savior. According to James, "every good and perfect gift is from above, coming down from the Father of the heavenly lights, who does not change like shifting shadows" (James 1:17). When God sent His only Son, He gave mankind the greatest gift of all—the opportunity to have eternal life in heaven and abundant life on earth—including the ability to have faith in the midst of change.

EVALUATING CHANGE

Again, as the French author said, "the only thing constant in life is change," but that doesn't mean we have to like it. Change can be annoying, confusing, even downright disruptive. But vigorously opposing change won't prevent it any more than sticking your toe into the ocean will stop the tides from ebbing and flowing. Use the following three questions to evaluate your own attitude toward change and what your responses to it should be. Again, it might be helpful to discuss your thoughts with a friend or in a small group of people. You might just find that you're not the only one who struggles with change.

1. HOW WOULD YOU DESCRIBE YOUR PERSONAL ATTITUDE TOWARD CHANGE, WHETHER IT BE ON THE JOB OR IN YOUR PERSONAL LIFE?

    Think about your typical response when unexpected (and not immediately positive) change occurs. Do you welcome it as a challenge, accept it with resignation, or resolve to oppose it with every ounce of energy you can muster? Why is this, and what, if anything, would you like to be able to *change* about your attitude toward change?

2. DESCRIBE THE MOST DIFFICULT EPISODE OF CHANGE YOU HAVE HAD TO CONFRONT RECENTLY.

    If you had been given a "mulligan" for that event—that is, an opportunity to respond differently, what would you have done differently, if anything? Why or why not?

3. HOW DO YOU THINK YOUR ATTITUDE TOWARD CHANGE REFLECTS
    THE CURRENT STATE OF YOUR FAITH IN GOD? BEING BRUTALLY
    HONEST WITH YOURSELF, WHAT ARE YOUR FEELINGS ABOUT THE
    REALITY THAT GOD IS IN CONTROL OF YOUR CIRCUMSTANCES—
    AND YOU ARE NOT?

It's been said, "I wouldn't mind change if only I could be the one to determine what changes are made, when, and how." Do you truly believe that God is sovereign and has your best interests at heart? If you do, but you still struggle with change, how do you think you might learn to exercise your faith to react to change with more grace and peace?

PRAYING *About* CHANGE

If you haven't experienced any major changes in your life lately, be prepared, because that is probably about to change! So use the following prayer as a guide for asking God to enable you to deal with change in ways that reflect His presence in your life.

God, to be honest, there are times when I wish You would consult me before sending major changes my way. But down deep I know You don't owe me an explanation for anything You bring my way. Please strengthen my faith so that I can trust the inevitable changes at work, in my home, in other areas of my life—and in society in general. Enable me to be a faithful, consistent representative for You in the way I respond to change so that others can recognize the difference You have made in my life and in their life as well.

Recommended Resources on Change

The Dance of Change, by Peter Senge, Art Kleiner, Charlotte Roberts, Bryan Smith, George Roth, and Richard Ross, Doubleday, 1999.

Fast Forward: The Best Ideas on Managing Business Change, by James Champy and Nitin Nohria, Harvard Business School Press, 1996.

Harvard Business Review on Change, Harvard Business School Press, 1991, 1993, 1995, 1997, 1998.

Leading Change, by John Kotter, Harvard Business School Press, 1996.

Who Moved My Cheese? by Spencer Johnson, M.D., Penguin Books, 1998.

Clearing the Confusion
About Money

Rick and Carol white-knuckled their way through another sermon on financial stewardship. Sure, they gave to support their local congregation, but they hated it when their pastor insisted on taking them on another guilt trip on giving. He doesn't have three kids who will be enrolling in college soon, they thought, and since his salary is guaranteed each month, he has no idea what it's like to live month to month on the uncertainty of sales commissions. "Let him lecture to the Hartwells," they said. "When her dad died, he left her a bundle, and Charlie is making hand over fist in commercial real estate. Now there are two people who should be cheerful givers!"

But despite their aversion to the topic, something in the pastor's message struck a chord that continued to resound in their hearts. "Godliness with contentment is great gain," he had said, quoting from the apostle Paul's first letter to his disciple, Timothy. That afternoon, as they enjoyed dinner at their favorite restaurant, Rick and Carol agreed that if there was one quality of life that they knew little about, it was contentment. They tended to get bored with the new car even before it was time for the first oil change. They had moved three times in the past seven years, always to a house that was just a little bit bigger and better, and in between moves, they kept busy remodeling the house they were living in. They never really stayed in a house long enough for it to become a home.

At the same time, Rick and Carol rarely responded to financial appeals, whether they came from the church or from another organization that somehow got their names from someone else's mailing list. "We're barely keeping up with our bills," they assured one another. "Let someone else support this project, someone who can afford it."

As Rick folded the receipt from their meal, he and Carol realized that they had some serious soul searching to do. They spent more eating out in one month than some people in Third World nations earn in an entire year. That new entertainment center and big-screen TV that they had been planning to buy—did they really need that? Wouldn't it make more sense to give some money each month to support two children in Guatemala than to buy another sport coat or another dress to put in a closet that was already jammed?

■ ■

It was a bidding war of ridiculous proportions.

Several years ago, before the boom for high-tech start-ups went bust, a home in a posh community in Silicon Valley was put up for sale. The list price? A mere $3.5 million—apparently a good deal in a market where, according to *Business Week,* the average price of a home had increased by 50 percent over the previous year. (How times have changed since then!) That 1.5-acre property attracted ten offers within a week. The eventual winner of the bidding war paid just under $7 million (yes, you read that right). What's even more amazing—especially to those in areas where the housing market isn't quite so tight—is that the buyer's plan was to level the existing home and build a new one.

This may be an extreme case, even for California, which often seems to pride itself on setting the highest housing prices in the nation. But at a time, in this area, when stock-option millionaires were practically a dime a dozen (or a nickel a dozen with options on a gross), it was closer to the norm than you might think. And while the real estate market seemed calmer elsewhere, the economic boom as a whole wasn't confined to the technology capital of the world—and it won't be at any time in the future, either. From Portland, Oregon, to Tallahassee, Florida, there has never been a time in recorded history when wealth grew more quickly and for more people, even after the run of unrelenting prosperity finally came to an end.

Although in the years that followed there was a dramatic correction, the facts of that period remain staggering. Fueled in part by the high-speed growth of e-commerce, the stock market broke one record after another. The Dow Jones Industrial Average soared past 11,012 points for the first time in mid-January 2000. It faltered in the following weeks and months, but the technology-heavy NASDAQ continued to surge, topping 4,800 points by early March of the same year. (To put this in perspective, when the current economic expansion in the United States began in 1991, the Dow was under 3,200 points and the NASDAQ was under 500 points.)

The rapid growth in the stock market sent the holdings of many Americans through the roof. According to various estimates, between 5 million and 7.9 million households had a net worth of $1 million or more in 1998 or 1999. That was up from 3.5 million households in 1990, according to Spectrum Group, a San Francisco research firm.

Wall Street's insatiable desire for dot-com ventures created many of these millionaires. Quest Software, in Irvine, California, for example, went public at fourteen dollars per share. According to the *Los Angeles Times,* the company's stock was trading above a hundred dollars less than a year later—a mere 631 percent gain from the offering price. By comparison, the newspaper said that it had taken the average New York Stock Exchange issue seventeen years to rise that much. "The Internet mania as we have seen it is redefining our measure of success," well-known Southland financial planner Victoria Collins told the *Times* in 2000. "It's no longer hard work and perseverance. It's being in the right place with the right stock at the right time. It's a whole new slant on life."

That new slant on life made traditional investment vehicles—viewed as healthy five years earlier—seem like underperformers now. Companies that didn't have a dot-com after their names were struggling to figure out how to survive in the tech-driven New Economy—and many of them still are.

In times of such great economic prosperity, it's challenging for even the most devoted followers of Jesus to maintain a healthy perspective on wealth and money. A consumer-driven culture makes it difficult to resist what Canadian pastor and *Christianity Today* contributor Mark Buchanan dubbed "the Cult of the Next Thing"—the propensity to "live endlessly, relentlessly for, well, the Next Thing—the next weekend, the next vacation, the next purchase, the next experience."

The church should be leading the way, guiding believers toward a balanced biblical understanding of wealth. But aside from an occasional sermon on tithing, the pulpits of America haven't provided much assistance to people who sincerely want to handle their money in a biblically based manner. "There are 2,350 passages in the Bible dealing with money and material possessions—more than any other subject, but it's the least talked-about subject in the church," Brian Kluth, the president of the Christian Stewardship Association, told *Kiplinger's* last year.

This needs to change. Believers in the church and in the marketplace need not view money in a negative way. But they must determine their approach to wealth based on what the Bible—in its entirety—says about it. There's no other way to effectively navigate through a money-oriented society.

The ROOT *of* MANY FRUSTRATIONS

Despite the incredible economic growth of the 1990s, not everyone cashed in on those boom times. According to a recent edition of *Business Week,* the median household income in 1998—$29,308—rose by 10 percent during the expansion. "But that leaves most incomes barely above pre-recession levels," the magazine reported. "And the gap between poor and rich is huge: The bottom fifth of U.S. households receives less than 4 percent of the national income, while the top fifth takes home almost half of it."

In addition, consumer spending and debt have kept up with the gains. Many people experienced unprecedented growth in their income or stock portfolios during the 1990s—and then lost it in the years following; so it's not unusual to find people in all tax brackets struggling with money on a daily basis.

We argue with our spouse when we balance the checkbook. We don't understand why our brother, father, cousin, or friend works far less and makes far more. We aren't sure how much we're supposed to give to our church and other worthy causes. We lie awake at night wondering how we're going to put our kids through college. We don't know whether we should put our extra cash in mutual funds or use it to buy a nicer home. We don't know how we're going to scrape together enough cash to pay for our daughter's cheerleading uniform or our son's basketball shoes. We feel an urgent compulsion to buy bigger and better gadgets and toys. We're worried about the future of Social Security and whether we'll have enough money for retirement. And the list goes on.

The varied, and often conflicting, myths that the culture (including the church) perpetuates about money only add to the confusion—such myths as (1) more money will make us satisfied and content, (2) we work hard for our wealth, and it belongs to us, and (3) money is evil. Seven or eight decades on earth is all that most of us get, so we need to make the best of those years while we're here; (4) therefore, God's sign of good pleasure on His children is to make them rich.

Such heresies are dangerous because they often contain a few elements of truth. As Randy Alcorn put it in *Money, Possessions and Eternity* (Tyndale House, 1989), "Without a sugarcoating of truth, the lie would never be swallowed." Take "prosperity theology" (also known as the "health-wealth gospel"), for example. Proponents maintain that wealth is a dependable sign of God's approval and that the lack of wealth is a sign of His disapproval. But righteousness does not necessarily equal prosperity, and sin does not necessarily equal adversity. Following God may or may not increase our bank account. Our income level depends on all kinds of variables, including where we live and what our job calling is. Some careers simply carry more income potential than others. A person who is called to be a junior high basketball coach or a truck driver can be fairly certain that he or she never will make as much money as someone who is called to be an architect or an anesthesiologist.

The FINAL ANSWER

Given the confusion and misunderstanding that surrounds the topic of money, it's no wonder the Bible has so much to say about it. It may seem that our culture is now more consumed with money than it has been at any other time in history. But people all over the world have been wrestling with the almighty dollar for centuries. This concern certainly made its presence known during the first century, when the Apostle Paul wrote his first letter to his protégé Timothy, the leader of the church at Ephesus.

As in his other letters, Paul gave very precise instruction about wealth and money in 1 Timothy. And the money-handling strategy he outlined for Timothy's congregation works as well for the twenty-first-century bookkeeper in Atlanta, Kansas City, or Phoenix as it worked for the first-century shopkeeper at Ephesus. Whether we're fighting with our spouse over the checkbook, struggling over whether our wife should work, or debating over whether our husband should get a different job so that he can spend more time with the family, the final answer centers on contentment.

If there ever was a saving medicine for our ever-consuming, ever-wanting culture of materialism, it can be found in 1 Timothy 6:6: "But godliness with contentment is great gain." The word *contentment* comes from two Greek words that mean self-sufficiency. In this context, this doesn't mean self without God. "The 'self' is not the origin or source of the sufficiency but merely the place where it is located," writes Ronald A. Ward in *Commentary on 1 & 2 Timothy & Titus* (Word Books, 1974). The term reinforces the self-sufficiency of someone who has discovered his identity in a life with Christ, as Paul had when he wrote, "My grace is sufficient for you" (2 Corinthians 12:9).

This type of self-sufficiency allows people to be content, regardless of their external circumstances (as we see in Philippians 4:11b-13). A content person can accept his or her station in life as being designed by God. A content person doesn't feel compelled to compare him- or herself with other people or compare his or her career and possessions with those of other people. A content person doesn't feel a constant need to chase after bigger and better possessions or achieve a higher, more prestigious position. Most important, a content person can focus on becoming more like Christ. And that, according to Paul, is the true formula for success.

The TEST

Contentment isn't something we're born with. As Paul indicated, it absolutely must be learned. And an education in contentment is open to everyone—although contentment is conspicuously missing from the list of skills that might be learned at Harvard Business School—or even in Sunday school, for that matter. Regardless of our circumstances, our upbringing, our professional background, or our family status, we can all learn to be content.

So how do we know if we need to get some continuing education credits in the study of contentment? The following checklist helps us test our level of contentment against the standard Paul outlined in 1 Timothy 6. (Although it's possible that some may be able to check every item, the majority will likely find at least one area that could use some improvement.)

1. WHILE WRESTLING WITH THE BOTTOM LINE, I FOCUS ON THE ETERNAL.

The ups and downs of the stock market often seem incredibly significant; many people devote considerable time to watching MSNBC and pouring over charts and graphs in *The Wall Street Journal.* But AOL's stock price at today's closing bell will be forgotten tomorrow. And no matter how good or bad our cash flow scenario is on any given day, it is absolutely irrelevant—in time and importance—compared with the vast stretches of eternity we face as followers of Christ.

According to 1 Timothy 6:7, "we brought nothing into the world, and we can take nothing out of it." Until we figure out that most of the things we focus on—Palm Pilots, stock options, professional status, and the like—are temporary, we never will find true satisfaction.

2. I KNOW THE DIFFERENCE BETWEEN ESSENTIALS AND NONESSENTIALS.

In any age of great consumption, such as ours, it's often extremely difficult to draw a line between what we truly need—for ourself, for our family, or for our business—and what we simply want. The fact that our earning power escalates during certain seasons of life and declines during other periods makes this assignment even more tricky. Many times, our rate of consumption is attached to our income rather than to a rational decision that caps our lifestyle and answers the crucial question "When is enough enough?" Typically, the more we earn, the more we spend.

Scripture offers a different perspective. 1 Timothy 6:8 states, "If we have food and clothing, we will be content with that." To the degree that we have too much or too little, we can find ourself in potentially dangerous ditches on either side of the road. (See Proverbs 30:8–9.) But God has promised to provide our daily bread. So when we're focused solely on what we need—to care for our family and help our company succeed—we can invest the rest into our community and fund God's work around the globe. Then—and only then—can our contentment flourish and grow.

3.   MY AMBITION IS SET ON SOMETHING OTHER THAN GETTING RICH.

We learn from I Timothy 6:9 that "people who want to get rich fall into temptation and a trap and into many foolish and harmful desires that plunge men into ruin and destruction." The picture here is of people saying—when they wake up in the morning and when they go to bed at night—"I want to be rich." But as this passage indicates, that kind of lifestyle is fraught with all kinds of traps and illusions. Money can be a means to an end—philanthropic giving, growing a business, and so forth, but if a person's sole goal is to increase his bank account, then he's treading on dangerous ground.

Remember the rich farmer in Luke 12:16–21? When his crop production exceeded his expectations, he decided to tear down his warehouses and build bigger ones. His passion was to accumulate wealth and hoard for the future so that he could take life easy. Unfortunately, his strategy had a fatal flaw: it failed to take God into account. In the end, he lost everything, including his life.

There are plenty of other wealthy people mentioned in the Bible (Abraham, Job, and Lydia, to name a few), but unlike this foolish farmer, getting rich was never their goal. Those who walked with God and were blessed by him didn't get rich merely for their own personal gratification.

Scripture offers several options that can replace financial wealth as the object of our focus. Proverbs 22:1 reveals that "a good name is more desirable than great riches; to be esteemed is better than silver or gold." And Proverbs 16:16 talks about how it is better to get wisdom than gold and to choose understanding rather than silver. Instead of having a deep desire to get rich, we should pour our energy into establishing a good name for ourself and for our family, into advancing in godly wisdom and understanding, and into developing impeccable relational integrity. Along the way, we might be rewarded financially as a result of our efforts. But that cannot be our goal if we want to learn how to be content.

4. I CONTINUALLY ASK MYSELF IF I LOVE MONEY.

Here's how an article in a recent issue of the technology magazine *Salon* began: "Money may be the root of all evil, but two religion start-ups are hoping to make bundles of it." The author probably didn't realize it, but he was perpetuating one of the most common misconceptions about what the Bible says about money. This illustrates how the meaning of scripture can be dramatically twisted by leaving out just a word or two. The misquoted passage in question, 1 Timothy 6:10, actually says, "For the *love of money* is a root of all kinds of evil" (emphasis added). Unfortunately, the myth that money is evil has been around for centuries; it has even been pushed in certain evangelical circles by people who assert that God expects the rich to give their money to the poor so that everyone can be on equal economic terms.

What about all the people who pursue careers in high-paying fields, such as cardiology, law, or information technology—not because they want to get rich, but because they believe that that is what God is calling them to do? Nowhere does the Bible say that these people are supposed to give away all their earnings to people who are called to lower-paying fields such as education or factory work. But they are instructed to be wise stewards of what God has entrusted to them. And part of being a wise steward involves guarding against the *love* of money.

The last part of 1 Timothy 6:10 reveals the harm that can befall someone who develops an unhealthy infatuation with money: "Some people, eager for money, have wandered from the faith and pierced themselves with many griefs." The phrase "eager for money" indicates someone who is struggling and reaching for money, someone who is focusing all his or her energy on making money. But the love of money can never be satisfied, as Ecclesiastes 5:10 reveals: "Whoever loves money never has money enough; whoever loves wealth is never satisfied with his income."

Many people assume that only the wealthy fall prey to the love of money, but that's not true. The sin of greed is the fire that feeds this unhealthy attraction, and its presence has nothing to do with the balance of someone's checkbook or the sum total of one's possessions.

Regardless of our income level, we should constantly evaluate our relationship. Answering the following questions can help us determine if we're flirting with danger in this area:

- What am I sacrificing to build my wealth?
- Do I treat people as tools to increase my personal wealth?
- Do I continually experience the exhilaration of quick fulfill-ment when I make a purchase, only to end up with buyer's remorse?
- Am I obsessed with my money, unable to stop counting it, sorting it, evaluating it, and so forth?
- Is my spiritual condition getting better or worse?
- Is my path littered with a consistent set of failures, relational or otherwise?

5. I AGGRESSIVELY ASSESS WHETHER MY HOPE IS IN GOD OR IN MY HOLDINGS.

As Paul wrapped up his first memo to Timothy, he gave a few last words of instruction regarding the wealthy entrepreneurs and business people in his congregation: "Command those who are rich in this pres-ent world not to be arrogant nor to put their hope in wealth, which is so uncertain, but to put their hope in God, who richly provides us with everything for our enjoyment" (1 Timothy 6:17). There always will be a certain degree of uncertainty associated with wealth. We can invest in the safest blue-chip stocks possible and do everything in our power to protect our holdings from economic swings, but we still could lose everything if the stock market crashed. The spectacular decline of many once-prized high-tech stocks is undisputed evidence of this.

Money *is* a vital part of life, of course. Consider what happens to an organization when money is short. Perpetual cash flow problems create anxiety, and if an enterprise is undercapitalized, the managers are often either under tremendous amounts of stress or they're living in a fantasyland. Thus, sufficient money can provide a stabilizing ef-fect for individuals, families, and companies.

But periods of economic prosperity sometimes lull us into for-getting about God. "One of the dangers of having a lot of money is that you may be quite satisfied with the kinds of happiness money can give and so fail to realise your need for God," C. S. Lewis wrote in *Mere Christianity* (Touchstone Books, 1996). "If everything seems to come simply by signing checks, you may forget that you are at every moment totally dependent on God."

On the flip side, if we place our hope in God, we reap benefits that money could never buy (1 Peter 1:3–4).

6. MY GIVING STRETCHES MY FAITH TO THE LIMITS.

The final ingredient in the recipe for contentment is giving. This doesn't involve a tried-and-true formula that says that as long as we give 10 percent of our net income, we're covered. It involves giving in a way that stretches us and makes our faith grow. The advice Paul had for the wealthy businesspeople in Ephesus remains true today: "Command them to do good, to be rich in good deeds, and to be generous and willing to share. In this way they will lay up treasure for themselves as a firm foundation for the coming age, so they may take hold of the life that is truly life" (I Timothy 6:18–19).

This passage confirms what the rest of the Scriptures teach: not that there's something inherently wrong with having money, but that we should hold our possessions loosely and be willing to share them with those in need. So how are we to give? According to the six keys outlined in 2 Corinthians 9:6–15, we are to give regularly, systematically, in proportion to our income, voluntarily, cheerfully, and sacrificially.

We are instructed to give, not so that we can gain God's approval but so that we can be a blessing to others. In turn, we will be blessed ourself—not necessarily with material possessions but with the priceless treasure of contentment. Paul provides the example in Acts 20:35: "In everything I did, I showed you that by this kind of hard work we must help the weak, remembering the words the Lord Jesus Himself said: 'It is more blessed to give than to receive.'"

The LORD GIVES, *the* LORD TAKES AWAY

We live in a time of plenty. Even when the economic factors may fluctuate more today than they did in the booming last decade of the twentieth century, most people still have more, not less, than they had ten years ago. Many businesses enjoy much greater revenue and profits than they had just a few years ago. In such times of prosperity, it's often harder to be content. But there is no better time than the present to *learn* how to be content.

Followers of Jesus are called to model a different standard when it comes to handling money. Whether we're struggling to pay the employees of our small business, flying high after a successful Internet

IPO, managing cash flow for a multimillion-dollar construction project, or simply trying not to exceed our departmental budget, we must demonstrate—in attitude and actions—good stewardship of the resources with which God has entrusted us.

We must also remember that there are no guarantees for the future. The economy could turn south at the drop of a hat (or at an announcement by the Federal Reserve). To keep things in perspective, we would do well to take a lesson from the ancient businessman Job, who, despite tremendous financial and personal loss, was able to say, "The Lord gave and the Lord has taken away; may the name of the Lord be praised" (Job 1:21).

The bottom line is this: we need to handle our money within the context of genuine and personal contentment—whether we have a lot or a little, have just inherited $10 million, or have just lost our business. Ultimately, everything belongs to God, and we must trust him to give—or take away—as he sees fit.

EVALUATING WEALTH *and* MONEY

Few topics can raise a stronger emotional reaction than money—especially if it's your own. Our typical reaction is something like, "I worked hard for it, I earned it, and I can do whatever I want to with it!" But that is not the perspective of the Scriptures. In the Bible, we find well over two thousand references to wealth and money, so we know that it's an important topic to God. Drawing from what you have just read, consider the following questions to assess your true attitude toward money and then determine whether you feel that there is any need for adjusting your thinking. Sharing your thoughts with a friend or discussing them within a small group will probably be very helpful.

1. WHAT AM I SACRIFICING TO BUILD MY WEALTH?
    Honestly ask yourself if you are sacrificing other parts of your life—time with your family, your health, or your personal well-being—to accumulate greater wealth. Do you treat other people as tools to improve your financial standing? If the answer to either of these questions is yes, do you think it is worth the cost? If accumulating a greater net worth is very important to you, why is it?

2. A RICH MAN ONCE WAS ASKED, "HOW MUCH IS ENOUGH?" HE
   ANSWERED, "JUST A LITTLE BIT MORE." HOW WOULD YOU ANSWER
   THAT QUESTION?

   What would it take for you to become content financially? Is there
   a fixed target you are aiming at, or do you—like so many other people—bump it up a notch every time you arrive at a previously desirable financial goal? Tell someone else where you think you are in this
   area and consider what steps you could take to strive for contentment
   that might not be influenced by your checkbook balance.

3. IF YOU WERE TO ASK GOD WHAT HIS OPINION IS OF YOUR
   MANAGEMENT OF THE FINANCIAL RESOURCES HE HAS ENTRUSTED
   TO YOUR CARE, WHAT DO YOU THINK HE WOULD SAY?

   We all see the value of investments—life insurance, stock port-
   folio, and perhaps real estate or valuables that appreciate over time,
   but how would you assess the investment you are making in endeavors that will make a difference for eternity? Do you enjoy giving to
   causes for the advancement of God's kingdom, or do you—like Rick
   and Carol in the opening scenario—cringe whenever someone talks
   about giving to the church or to other spiritual causes?

PRAYING *About* WEALTH *and* MONEY

Would this be a good time for you to pray about a sincere reevalua-
tion of your attitude toward wealth, contentment, and the resources
God has entrusted to your care? Use the following prayer as a guide-
line to get you started.

*God, with the uncertainties of today, it's hard to feel content with
what I already have. In a society in which we are surrounded by messages
that promote consumerism, it's difficult to distinguish wants from needs.
Give me the wisdom to discern between the two. Also, I deeply desire to
be involved in work that will continue having an impact long after my
time on earth is done. Teach me to be a "cheerful giver," and remind me
that I am just the manager—not the owner—of the financial resources
You have entrusted to my care. Show me how to use my personal wealth
in ways to make a positive difference in the world around me.*

Recommended Resources on Wealth and Money

Generous Living, by Ronald Blue, Zondervan, 1997.

A Life Well Spent, by Russ Crosson, Nelson, 1994.

The Millionaire Mind, by Thomas Stanley, Andrews McMeel, 2000.

Money and the Meaning of Life, by Jacob Needleman, Currency/Doubleday, 1991.

Money, Possessions and Eternity, by Randy Alcorn, Tyndale House, 1989.

The Roaring 2000s, by Harry S. Dent, Simon & Schuster Trade, 1998.

Spiritual Investments, by Gary Moore, Templeton Foundation Press, 1998.

Wealthy and Wise, by Claude Rosenberg, Little, Brown, 1994.

4

The Object of Our Ambition

After several years of sacrifice and hard work, Jim and Roger were about to realize their dreams. As best friends in college, they had talked about building a successful business together and how their complementary skills and personalities would make that possible. The company had finally broken into the black, and with several major contracts on file, the next year would certainly be their time to make it in a big way.

Unexpectedly, a headhunter contacted Jim about a key executive position with a multinational corporation he had always admired. But Jim felt torn: without him, Roger would be hard-pressed to keep the contractual commitments for the next year, but one of his long-held aspirations was to forge a successful career in international business. This was his dream job. How could he pass up the opportunity?

At first, he did not mention the job offer to Roger, but their years of friendship made such secrets impossible to keep. Roger couldn't pinpoint what was going on with Jim, but he could see that Jim was preoccupied and somewhat distant.

Finally, Roger just asked, "Okay, ole buddy. What's up? The last week or so you haven't been the usual, carefree Jim that I have come to know and love. You can tell me."

Feeling cornered, Jim hesitated, cleared his throat, and then explained the inner conflict that had him so torn. From the moment Roger grasped the situation, the disappointment and confusion showed in his face. Although he had been known to keep his temper on a short leash, Roger bit his lower lip, looked his friend in the eyes, and said softly, "It's your life, Jim. You've got to do what you've got to do. Just don't take too long deciding."

As he watched Roger walk from his office, Jim's face mirrored the pain. With a wry smile he thought, "Well, that sure wasn't any help!" But the question was simple: Was a possibly once-in-a-lifetime offer worth the cost of a once-in-a-lifetime friendship?

■ ■

Ambition is a concept best painted in word pictures, such as the following:

Ambition is Ebenezer Scrooge hoarding his fortune. A crusty grump, he cared only about squeezing a few more pennies out of everyone he met and everything he touched.

Ambition is Mother Teresa gently cradling an emaciated child. A wisp of a woman with stooped posture, she offered the world an unforgettable portrait of what it means to be Jesus to the poorest of the poor.

Ambition is Catherine the Great leading a "bloodless coup" to take the throne of Russia from her husband in 1762 and ruling until her death in 1796. Known for having multiple lovers, she also was responsible for reforms in education, health, and the arts.

Ambition is Max DePree rising to the top of Herman Miller, a multimillion-dollar furniture manufacturing company in Michigan. Perhaps best known for his books on leadership, he showed how a company could increase profits and employee satisfaction at the same time.

Ambition is Saddam Hussein invading the tiny desert kingdom of Kuwait. A ruthless dictator, he gambled the safety of his own people to pursue a personal dream of conquest.

Ambition is Elizabeth Dole exploring a run for the presidency of the United States. An articulate attorney who led the American Red Cross for seven years, she was for many years half of a powerful couple in the nation's seat of power.

Ambition drives one individual toward meeting aggressive sales goals and causes another to embark on a crime spree. Ambition sends some into retirement and draws others into highly productive golden years. Ambition is captured in fill-in-the-word phrases like "When I grow up I want to . . ." or "My goal is to . . ." or "I plan to . . ." or "Do you think it would be possible for me to . . .?" or "I have been considering . . ."

AMBITION DEFINED

Our English word *ambition* comes from two Latin words: *ambi,* which means "about," and *itum,* which means "to go." Put the two together and you have a concept that denotes a longing strong enough to make someone go out of his or her way to satisfy it.

Ambition is a sustained drive that springs from intense desire. It is a single-minded craving for something, which combines with perseverance over time to cause movement in a particular direction. Sometimes, ambition is like a raging river that runs a deep and wide course through an open landscape. In other instances, ambition more accurately resembles a slow trickle of water that inexorably wears a smooth path through jagged rock. In either case, ambition gets you there from here.

Ambition can be either bad or good. And it can be motivated either by the self or by God.

Paul writes about and illustrates ambition more often than any other New Testament author. He clearly acknowledges the existence and power of ambition, but he also draws an explicit division between self-ambition and God-ambition. "It is true," he admits to the church at Philippi, "that some preach Christ out of envy and rivalry, but others out of goodwill. The latter do so in love. . . . The former preach Christ out of selfish ambition, not sincerely" (Philippians 1:15–17). Later, the apostle begs the Philippians to "do nothing out of selfish ambition" and follows that plea with a magnificent description of how Christ allowed God the Father to direct His ambition as God the Son (Philippians 2:3–11).

But the same man who admonishes self-ambition identifies closely with God-ambition. Paul tells the Romans, "It has always been my ambition to preach the gospel where Christ was not known, so that I would not be building on someone else's foundation" (Romans 15:20). To the Thessalonians, Paul writes, "Make it your ambition to lead a quiet life, to mind your own business and to work with your hands . . . so that your daily life may win the respect of outsiders and so that you will not be dependent on anybody" (1 Thessalonians 4:11–12).

Prior to his conversion, Paul was driven by an intense passion to persecute and kill followers of The Way, thinking he was faithfully serving God. He had ambition. When he met Christ on the road to Damascus, he did not lose his ambition. But he redirected his zeal for serving the living God toward a very different goal. That transformed intention is obvious in his statement, "I want to know Christ and the power of His resurrection and the fellowship of sharing in His sufferings, becoming like Him in his death, and so, somehow, to attain the resurrection from the dead. . . . Forgetting what is behind and straining toward what is ahead, I press on toward the goal to win the prize for which God has called me heavenward in Christ Jesus" (Philippians 3:10–14).

AMBITION PERSONIFIED

Ambition differs from other biblical concepts in that there is no obvious place in scripture where it is defined and taught. Instead, writers of the biblical text most often illustrate its presence by describing what it looks like in different people. Some descriptions show God-ambition at work, as in the cases of Moses, Esther, Job, Gideon, Josiah, and Mary, the mother of Jesus. Pictures of self-ambition are not so pretty, including those of Lot, Esau, Jonah, Ananias, and Sapphira.

But perhaps the most precise portrait of ambition in scripture is shown in Solomon, the King of Israel. He hit the ground running and did not stop until he died. He built the spectacular temple in Jerusalem, constructed magnificent palaces and a great wall around that city, and amassed wealth that has not been equaled to this day. He also pursued pleasure, women, wine, and wisdom. The greatest kings and queens of his day called him great. His life is recorded in 1 Kings 1–11 and 2 Chronicles 1–9. His thinking is captured in the three books he authored: Proverbs, Ecclesiastes, and Song of Songs.

Solomon was a man of ambition. More precisely, he was a man of many ambitions. Some were God-ambitions and some were self-ambitions, including the following:

1.   TO RULE WELL: GOD-AMBITION.

At the very beginning of his reign, there was a defining moment. The Lord appeared to Solomon in a dream and said, "Ask for whatever you want me to give you." Solomon's request was as concise as God's offer: "So give your servant a discerning heart to govern your people and to distinguish between right and wrong" (1 Kings 3:5–9).

Solomon asked for wisdom so that he could rule well. God responded by fulfilling this request, plus much more: "Since you have asked for this and not for long life or wealth for yourself, nor have asked for the death of your enemies but for discernment in administering justice, I will do what you have asked. I will give you a wise and discerning heart, so that there will never have been anyone like you, nor will there ever be. Moreover, I will give you what you have not asked for— both riches and honor—so that in your lifetime you will have no equal among kings" (1 Kings 3:11–13).

During Solomon's reign, an endless stream of men and women, kings and queens, came to him for advice. Wisdom was Solomon's ambition, and according to the biblical text, his wisdom was as measureless as the sand on the seashore.

2.   To build: God-ambition.

God had promised David that Israel would be a great kingdom, and Solomon wanted to turn Jerusalem into a powerful capital city. He initiated the huge temple project immediately upon taking the throne, and he went to great lengths to see that this goal was accomplished, including signing a treaty with Hiram, king of Tyre, for the cedar logs he needed for construction (1 Kings 5:1–18). He built a great palace for himself, and he surrounded the city with a great wall. During his reign, the nation of Israel was transformed from a country of nomadic desert dwellers into a mighty empire, and the city of Jerusalem was the crown jewel of that domain.

3.   To pursue endless pleasure: self-ambition.

Solomon stopped at nothing in his pursuit of gratification. He testifies, "I denied myself nothing my eyes desired; I refused my heart no pleasures" (Ecclesiastes 2:10). During his reign, Solomon married seven hundred women and took an additional three hundred as concubines. That blatant immorality caused him great spiritual upheaval, which is addressed in Proverbs in the form of advice and in Ecclesiastes as reflection.

Life Lessons

Solomon is the personification of ambition—sustained drive that springs from intense desire. His life was a mixture of a number of ambitions— some motivated by self and others motivated by God. He lived out principles about ambition that we find taught in the Scriptures:

1. We have multiple ambitions.

Ambition relates not just to career and profession but to anything in life where sustained drive springs from intense desire. The biblical text makes it clear that Solomon had a number of ambitions—not all of them falling within the career category. But it is impossible to give intense focus over time to more than a few major priorities.

God does not always let us do what we want, even if we are sincerely seeking to honor Him in our efforts. For example, King David had an intense desire to build the temple, but God had another builder—his son, Solomon—in mind for the job (1 Kings 8:17–19). God has the freedom to direct our steps, which means that we must hold our ambition loosely within the context of His sovereign will.

We should not feel guilty about our ambitions and desires, as long as we are willing to let them go if God has other plans for us.

2. Ambitions are deeply personal.

Solomon had his own unique set of ambitions. He did not steal them from anyone. Neither has anyone else duplicated them. God makes us all in His image, but with distinguishing marks that set us apart from our neighbor. The internal forces that drive us that we label "ambitions" are often difficult for others to understand, precisely because these forces are so different from what others experience. Nehemiah left a comfortable job as being second in command to a world leader to become what we might call a start-up entrepreneur, rebuilding the city of Jerusalem. Peter was compelled to spend his ministry career working primarily with Jews. But Paul endured persecution and experienced shipwreck in order to tell non-Jews about Jesus. Both men preached the gospel, but to very different groups of people.

What causes one person to be an entrepreneur and another to work for a large corporation? What drives one college roommate to have a career across town while his roommate is unsatisfied until an international opportunity presents itself? Part of the answer to this question is *calling*. God calls us to our work. Ambition—again, the sustained drive that springs from intense desire—fuels one to answer that call. We can ignore that call for a time, but it will not go away. Understanding our calling is part of knowing what God wants us to do with our life.

3.   WE CHOOSE BETWEEN GOD-AMBITIONS AND SELF-AMBITIONS.

Scripture contains many examples of people who have demonstrated each type of ambition—God-ambition and self-ambition. In each case, they were faced with having to choose between the two.

For example, the Tower of Babel was an ambitious undertaking with a selfish motive: "Then they said, 'Come, let us build ourselves a city, with a tower that reaches to the heavens, so that we may make a name for ourselves and not be scattered over the face of the whole earth'"(Genesis 11:4–5). King Saul demonstrated an intense desire over time to get rid of David (1 Samuel 18:10–11; 19:1–17); Queen Jezebel had a similar drive to kill the prophet Elijah (1 Kings 19:1–2). And throughout the Gospels, the Pharisees and religious leaders frequently revealed their selfish ambition to murder the Messiah.

At the other end of the spectrum are Caleb and Joshua, the only two Israelite spies who were ambitious enough to think that God's people could take possession of the land of Canaan (Numbers 13:26–30). Nehemiah was willing to risk everything to rebuild the wall around the city of Jerusalem (Nehemiah 2:1–10). And the woman in Proverbs 31 is a picture of godly ambitions—in her business life, her family life, and her community life.

4.   SELF-AMBITIONS YIELD EMPTINESS.

Solomon built houses and planted vineyards. He made gardens and parks. He accumulated chariots, horses, robes, weapons, spices, and baboons. He bought slaves, procured great herds, and amassed huge fortunes in gold and silver. He delved into women and wine. Despite all this, he wasn't happy. His life was mundane, banal, empty, and "utterly meaningless" (Ecclesiastes 1:2b).

That sad scenario paints a compelling picture of what happens to a person who is driven by selfish ambition. No matter how high he or she climbs, there is no satisfaction or contentment. When the closing bell rings, it is not enough. The greatness of the accomplishment only highlights how meaningless the enterprise has been if God is absent.

Nowhere does scripture imply that there is anything inherently wrong with wealth, power, and fame. From a biblical perspective, however, those things should come as by-products of ambition, not as the direct objects of ambition. For example, Solomon's request for a wise and discerning heart pleased God so much that He also granted the new king riches and honor beyond compare (1 Kings 3:13). But Ecclesiastes 5:10 warns against making wealth itself a primary ambition: "Whoever loves money never has money enough; whoever loves wealth is never satisfied with his income. This too is meaningless."

5. GOD-AMBITIONS YIELD FULFILLMENT.

Nothing is more satisfying than living out a God-ambition. When internal ambition is linked with God's plan, life is good. That kind of activity and accomplishment will never be without meaning. The refrain that there is nothing better for a man than to enjoy his work is repeated again and again in Ecclesiastes. Indeed, Solomon makes it clear that the ability to enjoy work is itself a gift from God: "A man can do nothing better than to eat and drink and find satisfaction in his work. This, too, I see, is from the hand of God, for without him, who can eat or find enjoyment?" (Ecclesiastes 2:24–25).

Allowing God to direct our ambitions provides a sense of realism and flexibility that would never be present if our desires were based on selfish motives. Every enterprise has its ups and downs. What perspective, for example, does God-ambition provide for the bull market and the bear market? Ecclesiastes 7:14 states, "When times are good, be happy; but when times are bad, consider: God has made the one as well as the other."

God-ambition does not mean that life will be easy. But God-ambition always supplies a sense of stability. Remember Job, a blameless and upright man who feared God and shunned evil. If Job's ambitions had not been God-directed, he would have crumbled when he lost his considerable wealth and his family. Instead, he was able to respond, "Shall we accept good from God, and not trouble?" (Job 2:10b).

6. AMBITIONS OFTEN CHANGE DURING THE SEASONS OF LIFE.

Ecclesiastes 3:1 contends that "there is a time for everything, and a season for every activity under heaven." The verses that follow illustrate how various ambitions can wax and wane over the years: "There's a time to plant and a time to uproot" (verse 2a), "a time to tear down and a time to build" (verse 3b), and "a time to search and a time to give up" (verse 6a). This suggests that there also is a time to build a business and a time to sell it, a time to pursue an M.B.A. and a time to stop studying, and a time to raise a godly family and a time to enjoy the grandchildren.

Knowing that ambitions may not be set in concrete for life gives freedom to consider how God might rearrange our priorities and focus. Solomon concentrated on the temple, but when the temple was finished, that ambition was complete. It was time to move to something else.

The same principle applies to each of us. Out of the mix of ambitions that make us who we are, some might remain until we draw our last breath. Others, such as the desire to obtain an advanced academic degree or to assume a key leadership role in the church, may come and then go.

The CONCLUSION *of the* MATTER

Ambition always comes into more precise focus after the fact. If you put a group of retirees into a room along with a group of recent college graduates and ask everyone to talk about ambition, the responses from the retirees will generally be vastly different from those of the recent college graduates. When individuals are running their final lap in life, the desires that pushed and pulled them over the years are exposed for what they are: either God-centered or self-centered.

It was late in his life when Solomon realized that ambition apart from God was meaningless. At the very end of Ecclesiastes, he summarizes the topic with these sober words: "Now all has been heard; here is the conclusion of the matter: Fear God and keep his commandments, for this is the whole duty of man. For God will bring every deed into judgment, including every hidden thing, whether it is good or evil" (Ecclesiastes 12:13–14).

The challenge is to drive that biblical reality into ambitions early in the game of life. God-ambitions yield fulfilled lives. In Jesus' own word about his followers, "I have come that they may have life, and have it to the full" (John 10:10).

Evaluating Ambition

Ambition may start off as a neutral concept, but many of us throw it into drive shortly after we learn to walk and talk. The question is, where are we going? Are we blindly blazing toward a cliff? Has our engine stalled? Or are we soaking in the sights on a leisurely spin across the countryside? Here are three questions that can help you evaluate your ambitions. You can consider them personally, or you can use them for a small group discussion. After you evaluate them, write out your own course corrections and then find someone who can help hold you accountable by having you follow up on the changes you desire to make.

1.   What are my current ambitions?
    Be precise about the things that are really important to you. Make a list, and discuss it with a mentor or close friend who can offer some honest and insightful feedback.

2.   Are my current priorities God-ambitions or self-ambitions?
    Explore what is driving your ambitions. Be brutally honest. Ask yourself difficult questions, such as, Would the long-term effect of my ambition hurt others? or Am I overly motivated to please myself or another human being?

3.   What ambitions are missing and which ones need to go?
    Obviously, you will want to identify and eliminate unhealthy ambitions. But don't forget to add healthy ambitions. If you are married and have two kids but have no desire to raise a family, you might have a problem. If you spend six hours a day at the gym, working out, but you can't keep a job, you might have a problem. What ambitions do you think need to be reconsidered?

Praying *About* Ambition

Consider the following prayer as a guide to honestly seeking God's help in reevaluating and reshaping your personal ambitions:

God, I understand that I can make my own ambitions or they can come from You, but many times it is hard to tell the difference. So much in the world seems to "help" us determine what our ambitions should be. But I want my ambitions to be Your ambitions for me, because I know that only those will be truly rewarding and fulfilling.

Help me, God, to honestly reevaluate my ambitions for my work, my family, and my personal pursuits, framing them within Your guidelines. Give me the resolve to dispense with ambitions that run contrary to Your plan for me, to affirm the ambitions you have inspired me to have, and to discover those ambitions that will help me fully realize the potential that will bring challenge, joy, and satisfaction. Amen.

Recommended Resources on Ambition

Ambition, the Secret Passion, by Joseph Epstein, Dee, 1989.

Beyond Ambition, by Robert Kaplan, Wilfred Draft and Joan Kofodimos, Jossey-Bass, 1991.

Halftime, by Bob Buford, Zondervan, 1997.

Leadership Jazz, by Max DePree, Dell, 1993.

A Tale of Three Kings, by Gene Edwards, Tyndale House, 1992.

CHAPTER 5

Ethics and the Gates of Babylon

Christopher's company was facing a tight deadline, quickly running out of time to get their products ready for the spring trade show. His boss was pressing him to rush the design into production, without giving the client the opportunity to review it once more, as the contract stipulated. This particular design had undergone one revision after another. "As they say, Chris," his boss had said in a staff meeting, "it's easier to ask forgiveness than to get permission. We need to have it ready for the show and include it in the catalogue. We don't have time for Malone to look it over and then come back to us with more changes. They'll probably never notice anyway."

It wasn't just this particular project. Christopher and his boss were already at odds on several other issues, and the supervisor had given him the nickname "Moral Marvin," because he was a stickler for abiding by the rules. Standing his ground one more time could cost him that long-awaited promotion—and possibly much more. No time is a good time to be in the unemployment line, but with the news that his wife, Laurie, was expecting their first child, Christopher knew that the stakes of standing up for his principles would be higher than ever.

One impulse told him to forget it, that it was just a wallpaper design, not the secret for securing lasting peace in the Middle East. "If the client gets upset, we'll deal with it then," one voice in his mind told him. But a deeper conviction continued to nag at him. He knew that his integrity was also at stake. He couldn't be "reasonably ethical," making concessions whenever it seemed expedient, any more than Laurie could be "reasonably pregnant." She either was or she wasn't.

Coworkers in his department were well aware of his boss's affection for ethical compromise, and they admired Christopher for having held true to his ethical standards in the past, even when pressured. They were well aware of the current dilemma, and he knew that they would be watching to see how he responded. Finally, he realized that he had no choice about what to do.

■ ■

When George Bailey's ship finally came in, his ethical convictions kept him from climbing aboard. In Frank Capra's 1946 classic, *It's a Wonderful Life,* Bailey has the chance to make his dreams come true when his longtime nemesis, Henry F. Potter—the richest and meanest man in the county—offers him a job. The scene is one of the movie's most memorable: Potter calls Bailey into his office, offers him a huge cigar, and dangles a lucrative carrot in front him: Bailey could live in the nicest house in town, buy his wife fine clothes, and travel to New York and Europe. But there's a catch: if Bailey accepts the position, then Potter finally gets to shut down the Bailey Bros. Building and Loan— an institution that has been serving the working people of Bedford Falls for decades.

Bailey is tempted; he even asks for twenty-four hours to think about it. But as he shakes Potter's hand in preparation to leave, he has a change of heart. "Oh, no . . . now, wait a minute here, wait a minute," he says. "I don't need twenty-four hours. I don't have to talk to anybody; I know right now. And the answer is no, no! Doggonit!"

Despite his longing to see the world, Bailey turns Potter down. When he arrives at this ethical intersection in his life, he is able to draw from a warehouse of convictions he has been storing since childhood. Because of those convictions, he cannot allow his friends and neighbors to be mistreated.

Webster defines ethics as "a set of moral principles or values." For the follower of Christ in today's business environment, however, the definition goes deeper. It begins with biblical convictions—the foundation upon which ethical decisions are made. Housed within this solid warehouse of convictions for right living are the tools to make correct decisions at the rubber-meets-the-road times of life.

Ethics is a hot topic in today's business world, and it should be. The attention given to Enron and WorldCom certainly indicates a national ethical meltdown. In the 1990s, on the heels of several business scandals, many companies established corporate codes of conduct. The Ethics Officer Association, a national organization dedicated to promoting ethical business practices, has grown from twelve members to about 560 since it was founded in 1992. And universities around the country are increasing their emphasis on ethics programs in an effort to help students develop strong, well-established ethical convictions *before* they enter the business world.

Yet there remains a perception among some that business ethics is somehow separate from private morality, that our actions at work are not governed by the same principles that guide the rest of our life. In *Beyond Integrity* (Zondervan, 1996), Scott B. Rae and Kenman L. Wong point out that "many business people live with two conflicting sets of rules: one for business and one for their individual lives. In fact, when many alleged wrongdoings in the corporate world are brought to light, a common defense on the part of the perpetrators is explaining that they were simply playing by the unspoken rules of the game, rules that all interested parties were aware of and to which they readily and freely adhered."

Ethical dilemmas—and failings—are not a recent invention, of course. They were around in the 1940s, when James Stewart graced the silver screen, playing the character George Bailey, and they were equally dominant in biblical times. One of the most compelling examples of someone who based all facets of his life on God-centered convictions was Daniel, who successfully navigated a lengthy administrative career in a highly competitive, pagan environment with a number of different bosses without compromising his convictions or his commitment to God.

Daniel was born during the reign of Josiah, the last God-fearing king of Judah. From an early age, his mentors and leaders helped him develop convictions that guided him throughout his professional life. "It is justifiable to infer that the godly Josiah and the revival of true religion that had attended his reign made an indelible impression on the lad," writes J. Oswald Sanders in *Bible Men of Faith* (Moody, 1965).

"Since he was of princely or noble stock, he would be close to the throne and therefore peculiarly susceptible to the king's influence."

Once established, Daniel's convictions were tested in ways he never could have imagined. He was still a boy when King Nebuchadnezzar, the violent ruler of Babylon, invaded Jerusalem. It was the king's custom to bring the brightest young men from the countries he conquered to Babylon—not to torture them, but to train them to be statesmen. He did just that when he besieged Jerusalem, and "then the king ordered Ashpenaz, chief of his court officials, to bring in some of the Israelites from the royal family and the nobility—young men without any physical defect, handsome, showing aptitude for every kind of learning, well informed, quick to understand, and qualified to serve in the king's palace" (Daniel 1:3–4).

The young men taken from Judah in 604 B.C. included Daniel and three of his friends, Hananiah, Mishael, and Azariah, better known as Shadrach, Meshach, and Abednego. Under Ashpenaz's watchful eye, these boys learned the language and literature of the Babylonians. After three years of training, having been fully assimilated into the Babylonian culture, they entered the king's service. Unfortunately, their indoctrination also included a dietary element; they "were assigned a daily amount of food and wine from the king's table" (Daniel 1:5)—food that had been consecrated by a heathen religious rite. This may not sound like a big deal today, but for Daniel, it was a major ethical crisis.

It would have been easy for Daniel to make one little compromise; surely, God would understand if he ate the king's food. After all, his life was at stake. But Daniel "purposed in his heart that he would not defile himself" (Daniel 1:8, KJV). He didn't stand with his hands on his hips and defiantly refuse to do what he was told, however. He came up with an alternative plan. Imagine the scene: Daniel gets the chief official off into a corner and respectfully asks him for a favor. "Please test your servants for ten days: Give us nothing but vegetables to eat and water to drink," he requests. "Then compare our appearance with that of the young men who eat the royal food, and treat your servants in accordance with what you see" (Daniel 1:12–13).

Although reluctant, the official agreed to try Daniel's plan. The Hebrew boys passed the test with flying colors: "At the end of the ten days, they looked healthier and better nourished than any of the young men who ate the royal food" (Daniel 1:15).

Daniel's response when faced with this moral crisis provided the basis for a lifetime of quiet integrity. A man of profound learning and wisdom, Daniel quickly rose through the ranks of Nebuchadnezzar's regime and went on to serve in leadership capacities for several other pagan kings. He walked closely with God; in fact, as Sanders points out, he was "one of the most blameless of those whose biographies are preserved in Scripture."

Followers of Christ in the modern business world may never have to decide whether to eat meat offered to idols. Nonetheless, Daniel's life lessons about ethics and convictions are just as relevant today as they were twenty-six hundred years ago.

1. THE TESTS OF STANDING ALONE

The biggest test of a person's convictions comes when he or she is detached from a comfortable Christ-centered subculture. Given his background, Daniel probably lived a sheltered life back in Judah. He was surrounded by adults—parents, teachers, spiritual leaders—who encouraged him to seek God with his whole heart and soul. So it probably wasn't until he was jerked from his safe world and immersed in the pagan culture of the Babylonians that his ethical makeup was put to the test for the first time.

Daniel could easily could have blended in with his surroundings and gone along with everything he was asked to do. But Daniel had developed a warehouse of godly convictions so that he was able to make the right choices when he came to ethical intersections in his life.

Such tests are commonplace for the typical business professional. It's easy to talk about biblical convictions at home or in the shelter of a church small group, but it's not until we're faced with a sticky ethical dilemma at work that we find out how strong those convictions really are.

2. THE COMPANY WE KEEP

At times, Daniel appears to have been somewhat of a lone ranger when it came to taking the ethical high ground. But he surrounded himself with godly friends whose support made it much easier for him to stay true to his convictions. Knowing that his friends were behind him must have given Daniel courage when he was faced with having to describe and interpret one of Nebuchadnezzar's troubling dreams.

The despotic king not only wanted his wise men to tell him what he had dreamed, but he also wanted them to tell him what his dream meant. When the astrologers balked at this impossible request, Nebuchadnezzar was so furious that he ordered the execution of all the wise men in Babylon—including Daniel and his friends. When Daniel learned about this order, he asked the king for additional time to interpret the dream. "Then Daniel returned to his house and explained the matter to his friends Hananiah, Mishael, and Azariah. He urged them to plead for mercy from the God of heaven concerning this mystery, so that he and his friends might not be executed with the rest of the wise men of Babylon" (Daniel 2:17–18).

That night, God revealed the mystery to Daniel, and he was then able to provide the king with a full report of his dream *and* explain its meaning. The application is simple. We need to surround ourselves with people who share our commitment to biblical convictions and who are at least equally determined to live them out in practical ways. We need to find friends who will pull us up to higher ethical levels rather than people who will drag us down.

3.   THE POLITICS OF ETHICS

A display of firm godly convictions doesn't have to be obnoxious. Daniel is extremely graceful and winsome whenever he interacts with others who are at an ethical crossroads. When the commander of the king's guard came to find him after the other wise men failed to interpret Nebuchadnezzar's dream, "Daniel spoke to him with wisdom and tact" (Daniel 2:14). He was even gracious when he told Nebuchadnezzar that he would lose his throne and become like a wild animal. Of all people, Daniel knew that his evil boss deserved everything he was about to get, but he was still respectful when he broke the news to him: "My lord," he said, "if only the dream applied to your enemies and its meaning to your adversaries!" (Daniel 4:19b). And when he discussed his diet with the chief official, he wasn't demanding or disrespectful. Instead of informing the chief court official that he and his friends were going on a hunger fast, Daniel engaged his supervisor in a dialogue. He didn't just take a stand; he also offered an explanation for that stand.

People often ask what they should do if they work for a corrupt boss or one whom they can't respect for some other reason. They have two options: they can leave, or they can stay in that environment and demonstrate a life of personal conviction with discretion, grace, and a winsome spirit. Daniel did the latter—even though he had no reason to respect Nebuchadnezzar and the kings who followed him. In fact, he had every reason to despise them. After all, these were the very rulers who conquered the Jewish people, burned the temple, tore down the walls of Jerusalem, and stole the temple treasures.

Daniel's response to his bosses flowed from his faith in God. He served the ancient-day equivalents of Saddam Hussein faithfully because he believed that God valued every person, no matter how rotten.

4. ETHICAL INSTRUMENT LOCK

Ethical values must be applied consistently in all areas of life. There always will be people who will confront us, disagreeing with our standards. And we will bring some of that onto ourselves if we are not consistent. If, for example, we insist that all of our colleagues live up to our standard of sexual purity—such as not having an affair with a coworker—and yet we are often lazy and unproductive at work, we open ourselves up to criticism.

The tendency of some airline pilots to favor certain instruments over others is known as *instrument lock.* For example, some may rely heavily on the altitude gauge but check the airspeed gauge only occasionally. This obviously would not be the safest way to fly, because a pilot can be at twenty thousand feet and still stall and crash. To avoid instrument lock, a pilot must scan all of the gauges all of the time; he doesn't just check a few gauges that he's come to favor. We sometimes tend to focus on our own ethical standards—such as sexual purity, honesty, respect for others—while ignoring other ethical issues that may be more of a struggle for us. Avoiding ethical instrument lock means constantly scanning the environment—through the lens of a warehouse of biblical convictions—to make sure we're consistently applying ethical standards in all areas of our lives.

5. EXCELLENCE IN ADVERSITY

Ethical dilemmas or controversies are often viewed as obstacles to professional effectiveness. But the way Daniel handled ethical challenges was part of what made him such a valued administrator. It wasn't just the fact that he treated others with grace; it was also the fact that he made correct choices and demonstrated integrity at each and every ethical intersection. Under King Darius, for instance, "Daniel so distinguished himself among the administrators and the satraps by his exceptional qualities that the king planned to set him over the whole kingdom" (Daniel 6:3).

The Hebrew word for "exceptional qualities" means unique or extraordinary spirit. It has nothing to do with how strong or fast Daniel was physically. Instead, it has to do with his internal strength, his integrity, and yes, his ethical convictions. Daniel was really good at what he did, but beyond that, his heart was pure. His jealous colleagues tried to find fault with him, but "they could find no corruption in him, because he was trustworthy and neither corrupt nor negligent" (Daniel 6:4b).

6.   FAITH UNDER FIRE

It takes faith to hold to biblical convictions regardless of the consequences. Shadrach, Meshach, and Abednego faced the ultimate consequence when they decided not to bow down to Nebuchadnezzar's golden image; they were thrown into a furnace so hot that it killed the very soldiers who pushed them in. And Daniel's decision to continue praying to his God despite the royal decree that made such prayers illegal got him thrown into a den of very hungry lions. Had God not intervened, Daniel and his friends obviously wouldn't have survived these experiences.

We may not have to face lions or fiery furnaces when we hold to our convictions, but we could face other negative consequences. Coworkers might mock and ridicule us. We might miss out on promotions because we don't go along with the crowd. We might even lose our job because we stand up for what's right.

But we shouldn't naturally expect the worst to happen, just because we live an ethical life. Look at what happened to Daniel under King Darius. The king was concerned that his 120 satraps (we could call them middle managers) were stealing from him, so in an effort to cut his losses, he appointed three administrators, one of whom was Daniel, to oversee them. Why was Daniel chosen? Because the king needed an honest administrator, and Daniel proved to be exactly that. His ethical lifestyle had not gone unnoticed. In fact, on more than one occasion, Daniel was promoted, based on his past ethical consistency.

Shadrach, Meshach, and Abednego did not dance into the furnace, fully expecting to walk out unscathed, nor did Daniel snuggle up to the lions, secure in the thought that he would be having breakfast with Darius the next morning. These men had seen others die cruel deaths at the hands of the kings, and they knew that their decisions could put them in the grave, too. But their devout faith in God allowed them to face death without fear.

In today's marketplace, it's not uncommon for followers of Christ to fear the consequences of sticking to their ethical convictions. But if doing the right thing causes us to lose our job or our place in line, God has promised to take care of us. The big question on the test of life is not whether we have convictions or whether we know what's right and wrong; the question is whether we have an all-consuming love for Jesus Christ that prompts us to live—day in and day out—according to the standards He has set for us in His Word. That's what faith is all about.

7. PRACTICE MAKES PERFECT

Ethical behavior is not a last-minute decision. The principle is the same whether the issue is embezzling money from an employer, having an affair with a coworker, paying subpar wages, or cheating on corporate income taxes. If personal convictions aren't established before we get to an ethical intersection, it's naïve, if not downright absurd, to think that we're necessarily going to make the right ethical choice.

Daniel didn't wait until the king's official set a plate of forbidden food in front of him before he decided whether he was going to defile himself with it. Shadrach, Meshach, and Abednego didn't wait until they were called into a meeting and told they had to bow to the golden statue before they decided that they were going to serve God no matter what. These men may not have predicted the exact situation that they found themselves in, but they had established a set of godly convictions upon which they would base their actions. They had resolved in their hearts that they would not defile themselves. When they came to those ethical intersections, their warehouse of convictions held strong.

People who live out biblical ethics don't fill their warehouse of convictions by tossing around experiential and existential knowledge about this issue or that problem in a small group meeting. True ethical convictions are not rooted in preferences or opinions; they are founded on biblical standards. To maintain an ethical edge, we must shore up our understanding of scripture to find out what God says about honesty, fairness, treating people well, right and wrong, and so forth.

It all comes back to a personal relationship with Jesus Christ. Believers don't have to float around in a moral vacuum, fearfully wondering if the dam might break the next time the ethical waters begin to rise. The instructions for living an ethical life are clear: "He has showed you, O man, what is good. And what does the Lord require of you? To act justly and to love mercy and to walk humbly with your God" (Micah 6:8). If we fulfill these requirements, we can respond with the Psalmist: "Though you probe my heart and examine me at night, though you test me, you will find nothing; I have resolved that my mouth will not sin" (Psalm 17:3).

Evaluating Ethics

Expedience. Situational ethics. Whatever it takes to seal the deal. While these terms may sound fairly contemporary, the issues underlying them are as old as time itself. History is littered with the consequences of ethical compromise, and even in our so-called enlightened age, debate rages over what is right or wrong in the marketplace. And then, at Enron, a situation arises that draws attention to the problem all the more.

1. How would you assess the ethical climate where you work?

    Are there clear-cut standards of right and wrong, or do the guidelines seem to bend whenever it seems convenient? If one of your company's key core values and a big sale were at odds, which do you think would win out?

2. Have you ever been asked to do something that you considered unethical? What was your response—and what was the result?

    It has been said that the best time to make moral decisions is well in advance of a situation in which you might be tempted to act in an immoral or unethical manner. Have you tried to establish your own ethical "boundaries" in advance, or do you take the attitude that if the situation arises, you know that you will do what's right?

3. WHAT CAN YOU LEARN FROM THE EXAMPLES OF DANIEL AND HIS THREE FRIENDS—SHADRACH, MESHACH, AND ABEDNEGO?

Do you think that the moral stances they took would be realistic in today's high-pressured, competitive business environment? Why or why not?

PRAYING *About* ETHICS

If ethical decisions were always easy, we wouldn't need to pray about them—or wonder what we would do if they arose. Unfortunately, such choices are often difficult and the factors involved can be very complex, which means that we must pray and seek God's guidance all the more. Use the following prayer to stimulate your own petitions to the Lord regarding circumstances where you work.

God, I wish every ethical situation were just a matter of black and white, so that decision making would be simple. Unfortunately, circumstances are more often shades of gray—situations in which we might possibly justify actions and choices that may be questionable. My decision is to do what is best—what is truly right in Your eyes, not what is expedient and acceptable in the opinion of my peers or superiors. Give me the wisdom to discern what is ultimately best in every situation and the courage to stand for what is right. Help me be a "Daniel," not acting self-righteously but acting rightly as an ambassador of Jesus Christ.

Recommended Resources on Ethics

Beyond Integrity, by Kenman Wong and Scott Rae, Zondervan, 1996.
Business Through the Eyes of Faith, by Richard Chewning, Harper San Francisco, 1997.
Good Intentions Aside, by Laura Nash, Harvard Business School Press, 1993.
Intentional Integrity, by Millard MacAdam, Broadman & Holman, 1996.
The Power of Character, by Michael Josephson and Wes Hanson, Jossey-Bass, 1998.

Juggling Life Without Dropping the Ball

Robert enjoyed his work. At the end of each day he could look back with a sense of accomplishment, pleased to know that the many hours he was spending at work were paying off, both for the company and for himself and his family. Business was taking off, with every indication that the future would be even more prosperous, and he was earning more money than he had ever imagined.

Sadly, Linda didn't seem to appreciate all that he was accomplishing, even though there wasn't anything she wanted that they couldn't afford to buy. She had come from an affluent family, and Robert had promised to continue to provide for her in the style to which she was accustomed. "So what's the problem?" he asked one evening, in frustration after hearing another lecture from her about his coming home late from the office.

The problem was, at work, Robert could always measure how he was doing. Flowcharts and goals and sales and financial reports easily quantified whether things were going well or not. And, he was pleased to say, things were going very well. At home, however, it seemed that he could never do enough, and he had no way of measuring his progress as a husband and as a father. Even when he made the sacrifice to get away from work to attend one of Timmy's ball games, or kept his promise to go over to Linda's parents' house for dinner, there was no way of determining how well he had done. In fact, going to a ballgame only served to point a spotlight at all the other games he had missed.

"It's not worth the hassle," Robert thought to himself, as he struggled with conflicting emotions to prepare a good excuse for why he couldn't get away from work to join Linda for the party at the Wilsons'. He loved her and didn't want to hurt her, but there was so much going on at the company—good things—and now just wasn't the time to risk having something important slip through the cracks. "She'll just have to get over it," he decided. "There will be plenty of time for other stuff later, once things settle down here."

■ ■

On a recent vacation, Steve Graves and his family were exploring the streets of London, when they found themselves in Covent Garden, which is in the theater district near Leicester Square. Similar to the French Quarter in New Orleans but decidedly English in flavor, this area contains dozens of outdoor markets, vendors, and eateries, along with a diverse sampling of street entertainers—all vying for the largest audience. A couple of guys playing guitars entertained tourists in one area, while several violinists serenaded another group of onlookers. Children pounded on drums, and actors and actresses performed skits for whoever would watch.

These entertainers were interesting, but the most fascinating and colorful were the jugglers. One, in his quest to outdo the others and garner the greatest response from the bystanders, had strung a tightrope about eight feet in the air between two columns near the entrance of an old, abandoned church. As the crowd pressed in around him, he carefully walked the tightrope, juggling bowling pins, knives, sticks, and other objects as he went.

It would have been captivating enough to watch someone stroll a tightrope, but to see this guy simultaneously perform *two* precarious activities—both of which require a finely tuned sense of balance—was thrilling, indeed.

People are fascinated by jugglers for the same reason they're enthralled by watching an Olympic ice-skater execute a perfect quadruple Lutz jump or a gymnast perform a daring series of back flips on a balance beam. They're amazed at the balance and coordination such activity requires, and they're fascinated because they think they could never do it.

But, at least in the case of juggling, they may be wrong.

"Anyone can learn to juggle," Michael Moschen, one of the world's greatest jugglers, told the magazine *Fast Company* a few years ago. "It's about breaking down complex patterns and maneuvers into simple tasks. Juggling is a system of tosses and throws, of different patterns that, once broken down, understood, and mastered, can be put together to create something magical."

As the tightrope-walking performer in Covent Garden so gracefully demonstrated, balance is an essential skill in juggling. And, as Moschen points out, it's equally essential in life. But as the breakneck speed that characterizes the New Economy affects every area of our life—from our ability to focus on key tasks at work to our relationships with our family members and neighbors, it is getting more and more difficult to juggle everything and still live a truly balanced life.

The fact that many people are working from an incorrect definition of balance doesn't help matters much. Many followers of Christ have a hierarchical view of balance that involves ranking their priorities: God first, followed by family, church, work, and leisure. Unfortunately, balance is inherently impossible under such a system because it is based on an incorrect theological presupposition. It forces people to segment their life into categories and only focus on one aspect at a time rather than allowing themselves to live the fully integrated life that God intends.

Rather than ranking his priorities on a list, which implies that he must fulfill the first one before he can move on to the next, Gary D. Preston views them as pieces of a pie. "Each piece is important (or else they would not be priorities!); the challenge is not to keep them in order but to serve each area [as] an appropriate portion of my life," Preston, pastor of Bethany Church in Boulder, Colorado, wrote in the Fall 1998 issue of *Leadership Journal*. "For example, listing my first priority as 'God' suggests I need to fulfill my obligation to God so I can get on to the other priorities of my wife, family, ministry and, finally, community. Instead, in slicing the pie, I'm aware of all these priorities at the same time. Attempting to maintain equilibrium allows me to adjust the degree of focus I give my priorities at various times."

But what exactly does maintaining equilibrium look like? Does it involve placing all the pieces of one's life on a set of scales and trying to get them all to balance perfectly? Moschen doesn't think so. "Balance is not perfect stillness," he says. "It's the ability to make exquisitely refined responses to any unexpected change. It's the sense of little movements creating perfect-yet-temporary equilibrium."

That's easy to say for a professional juggler; after all, he spends his days honing his ability to make those "exquisitely refined responses." But is it possible to be a skilled *life juggler*?

The LIFE JUGGLER

One of the best biblical examples of a good life juggler is found in a familiar passage, but viewing this person in this way might require a major paradigm shift for some people. That's because she's known for being a "Wife of Noble Character" and a "Virtuous Woman" rather than as a model of balance.

This woman is described in Proverbs 31:10–31, and most Bible students think of her as the ideal wife. We're certainly not disputing that interpretation, but we believe that there is an additional application for both women *and* men. Aside from Jesus, there may be no better example in scripture of someone who demonstrated a finely tuned ability to juggle the balls of life. She didn't rank her priorities and handle them one at a time; she lived an integrated life, as the passage explains:

> A wife of noble character who can find? She is worth far more than rubies. Her husband has full confidence in her and lacks nothing of value. She brings him good, not harm, all the days of her life. She selects wool and flax and works with eager hands. She is like the merchant ships, bringing her food from afar. She gets up while it is still dark; she provides food for her family and portions for her servant girls. She considers a field and buys it; out of her earnings she plants a vineyard. She sets about her work vigorously; her arms are strong for her tasks. She sees that her trading is profitable, and her lamp does not go out at night. In her hand she holds the distaff and grasps the spindle with her fingers. She opens her arms to the poor

and extends her hands to the needy. When it snows, she has no fear for her household; for all of them are clothed in scarlet. She makes coverings for her bed; she is clothed in fine linen and purple. Her husband is respected at the city gate, where he takes his seat among the elders of the land. She makes linen garments and sells them, and supplies the merchants with sashes. She is clothed with strength and dignity; she can laugh at the days to come. She speaks with wisdom, and faithful instruction is on her tongue. She watches over the affairs of her household and does not eat the bread of idleness. Her children arise and call her blessed; her husband also, and he praises her: 'Many women do noble things, but you surpass them all.' Charm is deceptive, and beauty is fleeting; but a woman who fears the Lord is to be praised. Give her the reward she has earned, and let her works bring her praise at the city gate (Proverbs 31:10–31).

This passage provides a snapshot of what the internal and external customers in the woman's world thought of her ability to juggle her responsibilities in many different areas, from work and family to personal spiritual development and community service. In essence, it's a scorecard from her husband, her children, the people she did business with, the people in her community, and her employees—all the stakeholders in her world.

Saying that we are doing fine when it comes to balance is easy, but it means something more when other people say the same thing. This woman got high marks from the customers in all the key sectors of her life. In the family area, for example, her husband had full confidence in her (Proverbs 31:11), and her children called her blessed (verse 28). Her business associates recognized that she was a wise investor (verses 16 and 18), a conscientious employer (verse 15), and a hard worker (verse 17). In her community, she was known for caring for the poor (verse 20), and she was praised at the city gate for her "works" (verse 31).

Despite her many responsibilities, we don't get the sense that this woman was frustrated, overwhelmed, stressed out, or out of balance. Quite the opposite. Verse 25 says, "She is clothed with strength and dignity; she can laugh at the days to come." This incredible verse tells exactly what was going on in her heart and head; she didn't regret her past and she wasn't worried about the future. And it's clear from verse 30 that she had developed a reputation as a woman who feared the Lord. There was room in her very busy life for God, and the results were obvious.

The Proverbs 31 woman's example leads to a definition of balance that doesn't involve ranking priorities or teetering precariously on a set of scales. Rather, her life indicated that balance is *the ability to continually recognize and juggle the multidimensional assignments and opportunities of life.*

This definition is a mouthful. It took us a long time to develop and refine it, and we don't expect anyone to comprehend its full meaning after reading it once. So a thorough explanation is in order.

Examining *the* Definition

1. Balance is the ability to *continually* recognize and juggle the multidimensional assignments and opportunities of life.

Balance is not a static issue. We might figure out what it looks like for a certain period of time, only to have the picture change completely as our circumstances change. Balance in our life—or the lack thereof—can be affected by season-of-life issues, by month-to-month scheduling concerns, by family responsibilities, or by regular business fluctuations. To a public accountant, balance looks vastly different in November from how it looks in April. The same is true for the manager of a large department store who has to take a different approach to balance in March from the one he takes in the thick of the Christmas shopping season.

The downside of balance, according to juggler Moschen, is that people don't want things to change. But that's unrealistic. Constant fluctuation is the norm, which is why we must continually evaluate how we're doing. "The moment you've achieved balance, you'd better be ready and willing to get rid of it," Moschen says. "Because if you stay with what you think is perfect balance, you'll be far from in control. Remember, there is no perfect balance; there's only the approach to it."

2. BALANCE IS THE ABILITY TO CONTINUALLY *recognize* AND JUGGLE
    THE MULTIDIMENSIONAL ASSIGNMENTS AND OPPORTUNITIES
    OF LIFE.

The ability to recognize whether we are in a state of balance or im-balance is crucial, and it presupposes our ability to juggle everything in our life. If we don't know where we are, it's difficult to make adjust-ments, apart from a forced correction that occurs because we're burned out. In other words, living a life of balance begins with an awareness of all the many facets of our life and the impact they are having on us.

This is difficult to do alone, however. People don't always know when they're out of balance; it's not instinctive or inherent. When Moses—one of the best leaders the world has ever known—was single-handedly settling the disputes of the Israelites, he needed outside input from his father-in-law, Jethro, to realize that he was overloaded (Exo-dus 18). The same is true for us. We can go part of the way in figur-ing out balance on our own, but we need the perspective of our family members, close friends, and mentors to complete the job.

We all have blind spots, but we don't know what they are. If we did, they wouldn't be blind spots. So we all need another set of eyes to look at our life and help us see things we might otherwise miss. That's why we discuss balance-related issues with our spouse. It's why people have a business partner. It's why head coaches have an assistant. It's why companies have a board of directors. Being in the fray—wrapped up in product development meetings and game plans and personnel issues—doesn't allow us to step back and really evaluate what's going on in our life.

Many people get so out of balance that they literally have to sell their business, quit their job, or take a lengthy sabbatical to think about what went wrong. They take drastic steps to ensure that they don't get out of balance again, once they return to the heat of the bat-tle. Ironically, many people who try to solve their balance problem with a sabbatical actually resign shortly after their sabbatical is over. "I think it's because once they get away from the addiction of the work, they realize how nuts it was, and they don't want to live that way any-more," executive development consultant Caryn Joseph Siegel told *Fast Company.* Those who eventually return to the marketplace often do so very gingerly because they don't want history to repeat itself.

Such extreme measures might be avoided if people paid closer attention to what's happening in their lives. It doesn't take a month in a secluded mountain cabin; it could be as simple as scheduling regular times of quiet evaluation and assessment with a spouse or spending an hour every other week with a trusted adviser.

3. BALANCE IS THE ABILITY TO CONTINUALLY RECOGNIZE AND *juggle* THE MULTIDIMENSIONAL ASSIGNMENTS AND OPPORTUNITIES OF LIFE.

When it comes to balance, only focusing on one segment of life at a time isn't an option. That is the theological misnomer of the God-family-church-work-leisure hierarchy. The assumption is that we can take care of one area and then go on to the next. But a juggler doesn't use one ball at a time; he juggles them all at once. In the same way, we must simultaneously account for a number of different things.

"The death knell in juggling is to watch any individual object," juggler Moschen says. "Our instinct is to look at each ball or task separately, because we want to have control. It's a very insecure feeling: you influence something, and then you can't influence it, and then you're expected to catch it. But if you're tied to each little specific, you'll lose sight of the big picture."

Juggling isn't a skill people are born with; it's an art that has to be learned. Some people have a natural aptitude for it, but for others, learning to juggle—oranges or responsibilities—is a real challenge. People who are less skilled at juggling life's demands need to surround themselves with people who can help them.

This doesn't mean that we must constantly focus on every aspect of our life. Juggling life correctly is directly related to the span of time that we're addressing. If a person based her balance scorecard on a single hour and all she did that hour was work, she wouldn't look very balanced. Nor would it look like she was juggling work and family very well if she only looked at a three-day period when she happened to be on a business trip.

Juggling requires the ability to know that we have multiple balls in the air while recognizing that the ball we have in our hand—for whatever length of time—is the one we need to concentrate on. That's one of the enigmas of balance; it's a combination of concentrating on only one thing at a time while simultaneously performing multiple tasks.

4.   BALANCE IS THE ABILITY TO CONTINUALLY RECOGNIZE AND JUGGLE THE *multidimensional* ASSIGNMENTS AND OPPORTUNITIES OF LIFE.

Every person who has ever lived—including Jesus (see Luke 2:52)—has been multidimensional, and there are five dimensions of life that every follower of Christ is responsible for juggling: family, community, spirituality, work, and self. These are nonnegotiables. Regardless of social status, age, or professional position, every adult is held to this multidimensional standard of living.

These dimensions don't look the same for everyone. But we all have to juggle the multiple aspects of life all of the time, and we all have to make choices—sometimes very painful choices—in the process. Nobody can be in two places at once, so these choices are inevitable. Does a father accompany his very nervous child to his first sports camp, or does he instead attend an important strategic planning session at work? Does a manager work late so that she can make sure the project that is due the next day is as good as it can be, or does she take the time to go to her monthly small group leaders meeting at church? Does a busy woman go to the health club (to ensure that her body remains healthy), or does she spend that hour talking to her husband?

Taken individually, these decisions don't seem too overwhelming. But if we continually choose work over family (spending sixteen hours a day at the office instead of trying to be home for supper several days a week) or community over self (getting so involved in volunteer projects that we don't have time to work out), someday we could wake up and find that we're a heart attack waiting to happen—and divorced, to boot.

Obviously, there are seasons of life in which people must concentrate more on one area than another. When children are young, they need more attention than they do when they're at college. When people are involved in vacation Bible school, they spend more time at church than they normally would. When someone is finishing an M.B.A., he or she spends many hours studying—hours that might have been devoted to gardening or fishing. And when entrepreneurs are launching a new product or starting a new company, they'll work late for weeks, perhaps even months, until they reach their goal. The difficult part—during these special times of concentration as well as throughout the rest of life—is trying to figure out how to juggle everything without letting any one area suffer irreparable harm.

5. Balance is the ability to continually recognize and juggle the multidimensional *assignments and opportunities* of life.

Within each of the five dimensions of life exists a set of personalized assignments and opportunities, some of which are unique to each individual, and others of which apply to everyone. An assignment is something that we either have no control over or that we cannot say no to without violating a scriptural command or principle. As believers, we have no choice in the matter. We do, however, have a choice about opportunities. We can choose to accept them or reject them.

In the family area, for example, being faithful to our spouse is an assignment; sending a child to a school for the performing arts is an opportunity. In the church dimension, being connected to a body of believers is an assignment; serving as an usher on Sunday morning is an opportunity. When it comes to self, spending time every day nurturing our personal relationship with Christ is an assignment; playing golf on Saturday is an opportunity. In the work dimension, being called as a doctor, a fireman, a teacher, or a pastor is an assignment; volunteering to be on the company safety committee is an opportunity.

Of course, an opportunity for one person might be an assignment for another. One accountant may be called specifically to work for a ministry organization, in which case such a position would be an assignment. Another accountant may feel no particular calling to work specifically for a Christian company but chooses to do so because she enjoys the job. One person may be called to serve as an elder at church, whereas another views participating in the men's ministry as an opportunity.

And in the world of balance, some things can masquerade as assignments when they actually are opportunities. For example, a husband and wife may feel that working full-time is an assignment for both of them, when, in reality, they both have to work so that they can support their lavish lifestyle.

Some assignments—such as the sudden death of a spouse, the birth of a handicapped child, or the need to care for an ailing parent—dominate our life and leave little room for opportunities. These circumstances are never easy, but as believers, we can rest in the knowledge that God does not give people assignments without first equipping them—emotionally, spiritually, and otherwise. He never gives us more than we can bear (1 Corinthians 10:13).

Those who have not been given such assignments are faced with an ever-exploding range of opportunities. This is where life gets complicated. In the past, for example, if someone had a spiritual experience of some kind apart from regular weekly services, it probably came in the form of a special meeting at church or possibly a camp or weekend retreat. Now, the choices are practically endless—from Women of Faith conferences, Promise Keepers events, and marriage seminars to radio programs, inspirational concerts, and ministry-sponsored cruises, not to mention all the faith-based Web sites on the Internet.

Similar scenarios are repeated in the other four dimensions of life. We're bombarded from all sides with opportunities—often very good opportunities—that could help our career, enhance our family, or further the Kingdom of God. It's often difficult to choose, and it's often even more difficult to handle the ones we do choose. That's why the ability to recognize and juggle them is such a key element of balance.

Different people have different ways of dealing with this situation. On one end of the spectrum are those energetic, multitalented individuals who want to help everyone and can't say no to anything, which in turn prevents them from devoting enough energy to the best opportunities. On the other end are the people who fiercely protect themselves from anything that would impede their sense of balance, even to the point of missing opportunities that would be really good for them. Most of us fall somewhere between these two ends, and it's up to each of us to find the mix of opportunities that works for us individually.

ROOM *to* MOVE

The world of balancing life's demands and juggling the balls in all the various dimensions is pretty sloppy. It's confusing. And it's not the same for everybody. Once we get past the assignments we have in common, everyone has different options, and there's plenty of room for preference and latitude.

We're called to be accountable to other believers, but, ultimately, the question of what balance looks like in our life is a question we must ask—and answer—personally. We need to draw from the wisdom and insight of others, but when we stand before God and give an account of our life, we'll be on our own. We'll have to answer for all the time we wasted on unimportant things, for the relationships that suffered because we were off balance in one dimension of life or another, and for the lack of commitment we demonstrated in our personal relationship with Christ.

Although there sometimes is a need for biblical confrontation, it's not our job to judge other people's decisions and choices when it comes to balance. In this area, legalism, which results when we apply what we think God is telling us to other people, is deadly. It does two things: it makes us think that we know other people's worlds better than they do, and it takes away their responsibility for making their own decisions, which could make them think that they're no longer accountable for their decisions. Legalism has disastrous consequences because when we're talking about balance, we're really talking about how effective a person is in life. It's an overall scorecard of effectiveness.

On the flip side, there certainly are biblical boundaries that relate to balance within which we must live. We are instructed to live joyfully, without anxiety (Philippians 4:4–6). We're commanded to be a good steward of our time, our money, our talents (Matthew 25:14–30; Ephesians 5:15–16). We're called to work with excellence (Colossians 3:23). We're told to be attached to a community of believers (Hebrews 10:25). We're commanded to raise our children in the training and instruction of the Lord (Ephesians 6:4).

But inside these boundaries, we are left to figure out many things on our own. To do this successfully, one vital ingredient is necessary— a dynamic, growing relationship with Christ. Without this, we run the risk of falling into one of two traps: either we fall prey to legalism, believing that all we have to do to be balanced is follow all the rules to the letter, or we fall victim to a non-Spirit-led self-sufficiency, where we fool ourself into thinking that we have everything figured out and under control.

Only by having a vital relationship with Christ can we learn to balance our life as well as the tightrope-walking juggler in Covent Garden juggled his bowling pins or as well as the Proverbs 31 woman juggled the responsibilities in her world. And only by having a vital relationship with Christ can we develop the ability to continually recognize and juggle the multidimensional assignments and opportunities of life.

Pastor Gary Preston summed it up well in *Leadership Journal:*
"There will always be those who question any definition of balance,"
he writes. "But in the final analysis, I want to be a person and pastor
who can say, 'I have finished the race in all the events where God had
me entered.'"

EVALUATING BALANCE

The business leader looked up with a pained look and said, "I've got
it all together. I just forgot where I put it!" That comment reflects how
many of us feel as we work through a typical day—dealing with our
boss, our work associates, our customers, our suppliers, our spouse,
our children, our church, a volunteer organization, or a hobby or other
personal interest of ours. "Everyone wants a piece of me, and there's
only so much of me to go around" sums up how we feel. A balanced
life seems unattainable, but, deep down, we know that we owe it to
ourself, to our family, to our business, to our friends—and to God.

1. WHAT KIND OF "LIFE JUGGLER" ARE YOU?
   No one can live a perfectly balanced life 100 percent of the time,
   but do you feel that much of the time you manage to keep the various facets of your life in relatively good balance? If so, explain. If
   not, what seems to present your greatest challenge as you juggle life's
   demands?

2. WHAT STEPS DO YOU THINK WOULD ENABLE YOU TO ACHIEVE A
   MORE EFFECTIVE BALANCE IN YOUR LIFE? IF YOU THINK YOUR LIFE
   IS FAIRLY WELL BALANCED, WHAT ADVICE WOULD YOU OFFER TO
   OTHERS WHO HAVEN'T ACHIEVED THAT?
   Given your current circumstances—the demands of your job,
   your family responsibilities and expectations, and so forth, is the idea
   of achieving a degree of proper balance even realistic? If not, can you
   see a time in the not-too-distant future when that might change? If
   you feel limited to a perpetually out-of-balance existence, would you
   be willing to make necessary changes to make a better balance in life
   possible?

3. AS YOU HAVE ADDRESSED THE CHALLENGE OF JUGGLING LIFE'S
    DEMANDS, WHAT HAS BEEN THE IMPACT ON YOUR RELATIONSHIP
    WITH GOD? TO ASK THE QUESTION ANOTHER WAY, HOW HAS
    YOUR RELATIONSHIP WITH GOD AFFECTED YOUR ABILITY TO
    JUGGLE LIFE'S DEMANDS?

If your life is out of balance, could it be that a key to resolving this problem is to develop a deeper, more intimate relationship with God? You might think, "My life is so complicated now, I just don't have time to spend with God!" But could it be that by making Him a priority, He might enable you to begin getting other aspects of your life in order?

PRAYING *About* BALANCE

When our life is out of balance, we tend to feel guilt, frustration, anger, and, sometimes, even hopelessness. But hope is one of the great benefits of a growing, fruitful relationship with God. If you're wrestling with any of the emotions previously mentioned, the suggested prayer that follows may help you present your need to God. If things seem fairly ordered for you right now, you still need this prayer, because things can suddenly change, causing your carefully cultivated sense of balance to be disrupted.

God, someone has said that the only person he ever saw in balance was the individual who was simply moving from one extreme to the other. I often feel that way, getting overcommitted in one area and trying to adjust, only to lean too far in another direction. Jesus Christ seemed always to manage to keep His life in order despite the chaos that surrounded Him. The Scriptures enable me to use the mind of Christ to evaluate my life's circumstances and make the needed adjustments. I know that trying to be all things to all people is futile, but empower me to be all that You want me to be.

Recommended Resources on Balance

Beating Burnout, by Frank Minirth, Paul Meier, Don Hawkins, Chris Thurman, and
    Richard Flournoy, Budget Book Service, 1997.
Boundaries, by Henry Cloud and John Townsend, Zondervan, 1992.

Harvard Business Review on Work and Life Balance, compilation by various authors, Harvard Business School Press, 2000.

If Life Is a Balancing Act, Why Am I So Darn Clumsy? by Dick Biggs, Chattahoochee, 1993.

Ordering Your Private World, by Gordon MacDonald, Nelson, 1997.

The Overload Syndrome, by Richard Swenson, NavPress, 1999.

Tyranny of the Urgent, by Charles Hummel, InterVarsity, 1994.

The Forgotten Role of Stewardship

Without question, Richard was a gifted businessman. During his career, he had started a number of enterprises and each had become profitable within a short time. A couple of them he had hung onto, but the rest he had been able to sell at a considerable profit. He was both innovative and able to implement the cutting-edge ideas that came to him, seemingly from out of nowhere.

Friends marveled at Richard's success. "You could touch manure and it would turn into gold," quipped one of his business partners. Richard would just smile and accept the compliment, but deep down he was just as amazed as his counterparts. If someone had asked him, "How do you do it?" he would have been at a loss to provide a credible answer. He had worked hard in college, graduating with honors, and during his early years in business he had received excellent mentoring from some very experienced, accomplished business executives. But so had some of his college buddies, yet they had not attained nearly the level of success that he had, so there was more to it than that.

One day, the business reporter from the local newspaper interviewed him for a feature article. When the reporter asked, "What's the secret of your success?" Richard shrugged and responded humbly, "I really don't know. I guess it's just a God-given ability."

Later in the day, that answer continued to echo in Richard's mind. If God truly has given me the ability to start and develop successful businesses, he thought, why did He do that? And what does He expect from me in return? During his devotional time one morning, Richard decided to spend some time researching the biblical concept of stewardship. Realizing that one of the responsibilities of a good steward is to manage those things placed under his or her care in a way that will please the owner, he began wondering how God as the owner would rate his stewardship.

Until that time, if someone had asked how well he was serving the Lord, Richard would have answered that he was doing fairly well. After examining the Scriptures, however, he wasn't nearly as certain. Yes, he regularly tithed from his income—off the gross, not the net. And he regularly attended church and devoted many hours to his congregation, serving on several committees in a variety of roles. That was a good start, but . . .

Richard thought of the employees entrusted to his care, including his leadership team. Was he providing for their needs as best he could, not only in direct compensation but also in benefits? Was he providing an environment in which they each could grow professionally and personally, enabling them to flourish in their current jobs and fully use their skills and abilities?

He also considered his witness as a business leader who also follows Jesus Christ: Had he made it clear to others that Jesus was the center of his life, and had he taken advantage of opportunities to "give an answer to anyone who asks the reason for the hope" that he had, as 1 Peter 3:15 exhorts?

What about his family? Was he becoming a husband and father who more and more reflected the love and grace of Christ to his wife and children? They enjoyed a spacious home with every convenience imaginable, but Richard suddenly realized that they had not been as eager to share that blessing with others—through hospitality events or even through housing visits—as they should have been.

"I really want to be a good steward, Lord," he admitted in a brief prayer, "but I can see now that I have a long way to go!"

■ ■

Stewardship rates barely an honorable mention in the lexicon of current business terminology. A scan of cover stories in *Fortune, Forbes,*

Fast Company, and *Harvard Business Review* for the last three years revealed that leadership was featured in twelve instances, change was covered on four occasions, work was the leading topic seven times, and strategy was explored in a total of fifty-seven issues. Stewardship was completely ignored.

In a group of professionals, ask the leaders or owners to stand up. There will be lots of movement in the room as men and women get to their feet. Then ask the stewards to raise their hands. Not much will happen; people might even look at each other with confused looks. People do not readily identify themselves as stewards.

A steward is one who protects and adds value to assets placed under his or her control by the owner of those assets. Stewards manage property, people, and resources that they themselves do not own. A steward is like the caretaker of an estate, who oversees the entire property, including employees, gardens, financial accounts, maintenance, expansion, and all business affairs. A steward serves the owner and is accountable to the owner for the well-being of the assets placed under his or her care.

Our business environment evaluates opportunities primarily through the lens of ownership. What is my profit sharing plan? What kind of stock options will I accumulate? If I don't own a piece of the action—somehow, I will lose motivation and incentive. I will not be able to give you my best.

But scripture leans heavily on the concept of stewardship to explain professional life. Is stewardship out of date and irrelevant to current best practices? Or is it still relevant and we just don't know it?

Properly understood, stewardship is far more significant as a practice than as a mere word or as just another good idea. The concept is deeply anchored in theology, having first been introduced in the inaugural chapters of Genesis. Stewardship is therefore as old as creation, and three simple truths summarize both its definition and its magnificence (Genesis 1:26–30):

1. God created and therefore He owns.

2. We manage resources that God owns.

3. We were created in God's image and therefore are expected to manage resources the way God would manage them.

God delegates to us the management of His resources. We are His agents, His ambassadors. We possess His power of attorney for management decision making. God has entrusted us with representing His mind and with seeking to mirror the action we believe He would take—across the entire bandwidth of our stewardship continuum. This includes our responsibilities for people, profit and loss, use of cash, and the implementation of good core values. Stewardship plays a vital role in negotiations and communication, as well as in our dealings with customers and suppliers.

We leave Genesis 2 with a term that is clothed in divine majesty and gives clear instruction for our oversight of resources. We are *stewards*. Our bottom line is very clear: as followers of Christ, we own nothing—except salvation and our name. Everything else belongs to God. We can pretend to own our bank account, our family, our intelligence, our mix of spiritual gifts, our skills, our stocks, and our job. But in reality, these are all assets under our control that we do not own.

How does that understanding of stewardship translate into our work environment?

Jesus often spoke in word pictures, and one of His parables is of an incompetent steward—or shrewd manager. To his disciples, Jesus tells the story of a steward who did a poor job and was fired as a consequence:

> There was a rich man whose manager was accused of wasting his possessions. So he called him in and asked him, "What is this I hear about you? Give an account of your management, because you cannot be manager any longer."
>
> The manager said to himself, "What shall I do now? My master is taking away my job. I'm not strong enough to dig, and I'm ashamed to beg—I know what I'll do so that when I lose my job here, people will welcome me into their houses."
>
> So he called in each one of his master's debtors. He asked the first, "How much do you owe my master?"
>
> "Eight hundred gallons of olive oil," he replied.
>
> The manager told him, "Take your bill, sit down quickly, and make it four hundred."
>
> Then he asked the second, "And how much do you owe?"

"A thousand bushels of wheat," he replied.

He told him, "Take your bill and make it eight hundred."

The master commended the dishonest manager because he had acted shrewdly. For the people of this world are more shrewd in dealing with their own kind than are the people of the light.

Whoever can be trusted with very little can also be trusted with much, and whoever is dishonest with very little will also be dishonest with much (Luke 16:1–8,10).

From this account, the following principles regarding stewardship emerge:

1. STEWARDSHIP IS KNOWING THE DIFFERENCE BETWEEN BEING AN OWNER AND BEING A CARETAKER.

Stewardship begins with the realization that everything I have was given to me—and ownership still remains in God's name. My paycheck, my business, my employees, my employers, my money, my gifts, my children, my house, my job, my body, my intellect, my emotions, my car, my toys, my hobbies, my strengths—all are on loan from God.

As such, stewardship is a philosophy that should permeate all of life and business. This approach begins on the inside, governing the way a person thinks, sees, and feels—including his or her motivation, and then it ultimately works itself out into external physical structures, assets, and opportunities.

Steve Graves has a friend who for years has taken his Christmas bonus, a check for more than ten thousand dollars, to the bank, asking that he receive the money in hundred-dollar bills. He then distributes the money anonymously, placing it in the mailboxes of families who he knows are in need. He has come to grips with the fact that his possessions are not really his.

Steve will never forget the first time his friend did this. It was early in December and his friend called him, asking if he would be willing to help him in delivering some "Christmas cheer" to some families in Northwest Arkansas. Knowing his friend very well, Steve readily agreed. "How can I help?" Steve asked.

Steve's friend asked him if he would compile a list of everyone he knew, to whom a little extra money would make a huge difference in the quality of his or her Christmas celebration. Steve came up with a list of thirty to forty people, including college students, single parents, and families who had suffered health or financial setbacks.

One evening, Steve's friend picked him up in his car and they drove around to the home of each person on his list, as well as to the homes of the people Steve had listed. Steve's friend had placed hundred-dollar bills in envelopes, along with a typed note about the good news of Christmas, explaining that the money he was sharing with them was not his—that it had merely been placed in his car, on loan from God, in a sense.

Steve was amazed at his friend's generosity. Steve wondered how he would have responded if he had received a similar windfall of extra income.

Stewardship, however, does not necessarily mean that we give all our money away. It does absolutely mean that we care for the assets under our control the way God Himself would manage them. He is the owner. We are only His stewards. In his sermon titled "The Good Steward," John Wesley addressed that issue eloquently in the eighteenth century: "We are not at liberty to use what He has lodged in our hands as we please, but as He pleases who alone is possessor of heaven and earth, and the Lord of every creature. We have no right to dispose of anything we have, but according to His will, seeing we are not proprietors of any of these things."

2.   STEWARDSHIP IS MEASURABLE PERFORMANCE THAT IS OPEN FOR EVALUATION.

Stewardship inherently involves evaluation of performance. Owners have a right to ask, and stewards have an obligation to respond. Assessment and accountability come with the territory for stewards.

According to the parable, the owner received his report regarding mismanagement from a third party. He asked the steward, "What is this I hear about you?" The owner requested that the steward give an account of the results of his stewardship and immediately made a judgment regarding continued employment.

Evaluation is critical for a steward. Sometimes, that takes the form of self-reflection. For instance, for years, we have made it a practice to take time over the Christmas holidays for personal contemplation. We ask ourselves a series of questions, such as, How am I doing with my friends? What are my spiritual gifts and how are they being used? What are the danger areas currently facing my life? How did I do with last year's opportunities, and how will I be positioned to face next year's opportunities? Am I on target with my life mission?

Evaluation at other times has a more public edge—such as in project and proposal reviews, at meetings before the board of directors, or in sessions in the boss's office. Such words as *critique, review, evaluate, assess, study,* and *examine* tell the story of what the life of a steward looks like throughout the ebb and flow of his or her professional life.

But the scrutiny of our stewardship goes even further than self-evaluation and assessment by others. God, who gave us the title of steward in the first place, is constantly aware of our stewarding choices and will ask us to give an account regarding our performance, actions, and results. Paul explains it as follows:

> By the grace God has given me, I laid a foundation as an expert builder, and someone else is building on it. But each one should be careful how he builds. For no one can lay any foundation other than the one already laid, which is Jesus Christ. If any man builds on this foundation using gold, silver, costly stones, wood, hay or straw, his work will be shown for what it is, because the Day will bring it to light. It will be revealed with fire, and the fire will test the quality of each man's work. If what he has built survives, he will receive his reward. If it is burned up, he will suffer loss; he himself will be saved, but only as one escaping through the flames (1 Corinthians 3:10–15).

In the business environment, we have a variety of means for measuring the results of our investments and efforts. We talk in terms of ROI (return on investment), ROA (return on assets), and ROE (return on equity). But as we consider Jesus' parable of the wise steward, it seems that we need to redefine the method of measuring our personal stewardship. We would suggest thinking in terms of ROSA (return on stewardship assets), which involves not only money, but also our time, gifts, skills, experience, and anything else God has entrusted to our care. What have we done with what He has given to us as His caretakers?

There is one other contrast between stewardship in a business sense and stewardship in spiritual terms. Typically, the return in business can be evaluated by a profit and loss statement, by increased or decreased sales, and by other quantifiable measurements. However, the outcome from spiritual investments is harder to measure; sometimes, it can't be calculated at all. For instance, when Steve's friend gave the anonymous gifts, he trusted that he was responding to God's leading, without any guarantee that the money in each case would be used in a manner that the Lord would find acceptable. Being a good steward of God's resources is often simply a matter of doing as He directs and leaving the outcome up to Him.

But whether we ever see or know the results, we can be assured that the daily decisions we make as stewards literally reverberate into eternity. After all our performance evaluations are over, we still have one more to sit through. God wants to talk—and we will listen. Stewardship means performance that is open for evaluation, whether it can be measured in human terms or not.

3.   STEWARDSHIP IS PROTECTING AND GROWING THE OWNER'S ASSETS WITH FIERCE INTENSITY.

Jesus' stewardship parable is a striking contrast between two sets of actions. At first, the steward is called to account for being wasteful, and then the owner later compliments the steward for acting shrewdly.

What happened in between? When the owner gave the steward his two-week termination notice, the steward immediately went to work. All of a sudden, the steward was focused like a laser on the assets under his care. He figured out very quickly how to maximize their benefits and returns. He put those resources to work.

One can almost read the owner's mind as he watches this flurry of activity; the owner is thinking, *What's up with that? Where did all this initiative come from? Where did he find this incredible reservoir of energy?* Even though the steward's activity was purely selfish, the owner praised him for demonstrating the intense concentration, ambition, and hustle that should have been present all along. Unspoken in the text is what the owner must have been thinking: *You are really good at this. You could teach graduate-level courses on being a steward. Too bad you weren't willing to do for me what you did for yourself.*

In just a few words, Jesus paints a picture of the options available for a steward's performance. At one end of the continuum, the steward is careless, reckless, and wasteful with assets and opportunities. At the other end of the spectrum, the steward handles everything under his or her care shrewdly, wisely, artfully, and astutely.

The work of a steward is like that of managers of large investment funds. They take money that has been entrusted to them—but does not belong to them—and then spend every ounce of their intellect and creativity to protect and grow that asset. They watch the stock and bond markets with unrelenting attention. They dream about the market at night. They are driven to make the funds under their care grow. They are stewards.

4. STEWARDSHIP IS DETERMINED BY HOW SMALL THINGS ARE HANDLED.

A reporter asked the CEO of a highly regarded amusement park what accounted for the attraction's success. The executive's answer was simple: cigarette butts. The park's staff was instructed to let discarded cigarettes remain on the ground for no more than thirty seconds. The leader explained the unusual policy by contending that you prove your ability to handle big things by how you handle small things. That is good business as well as good theology.

The following is a truth that consistently threads its way through scripture: Do good work with less before you can expect to be given more. Why? Because handling small projects, or little money, or few people with success establishes a disciplined approach to doing the same thing on a larger scale. In life, there is no substitute for experience. Someone who properly controls a $1 million budget will most likely also do well overseeing $100 million.

Our culture ascribes little value to giving attention to anything small. We prefer challenges that are robust, customer accounts that are global, a large span of control, and national exposure. Good stewards spend little time seeking something greater to manage. They are focused instead on handling the details of what they already have been asked to oversee.

Several years ago, Steve Graves was helping to raise money for a nonprofit charitable organization. He had asked to meet with a couple he knew very well—both physicians, working together in their own practice—to see if they would be willing to give to this worthy cause.

As Steve explained the need, they made an interesting comment. One of them had just received a raise in salary and both of them had been asking God what He wanted them to do with the additional money. Being affluent doesn't necessarily mean that one has "enough," so Steve was amazed—and encouraged—to hear that this successful couple wanted to know how best to use their extra resources for the Kingdom's purposes, rather than using it to satisfy another "want."

Without a doubt, God's proving ground for stewardship's effectiveness is in how the small things are handled.

5. STEWARDSHIP IS BUILT AND MAINTAINED ON TRUST.

Ancient literature often pictured the steward as the manager of a large, sprawling estate. It was the job of the steward to stand in for the estate owner during the owner's absence because of business travel or war duty. Whether the owner was gone for a week or a year, the steward was responsible for protecting and growing the value of everything within the boundaries of the estate. The owner placed all of his trust in the steward.

At the core of stewardship is this covenant of trust. Owners only relinquish control when trust flows from them to the steward. One synonym for stewardship is *trusteeship,* which inherently summarizes the kind and quality of relationship that needs to exist between the owner and the steward. This relationship concerns such issues as motives, the process for completing tasks, the philosophy of leadership, attention to detail, communication style, the use of authority, values, and work ethic.

Stewardship is impossible without trust. It is more than a label; it's a framework for living. A proper understanding of stewardship allows an individual to move from being an aggressive accumulator of assets—along with all the stress associated with that orientation—to being a willing acceptor of assets God wishes to place under his or her control. In other words, stewardship gives us the luxury of giving focused attention to the assets we have been given, rather than devoting energy to acquiring more.

We are all stewards. For each of us, this title is the same, even though we have been given different assets, resources, property, and other valuables to oversee. Our responsibility is to be faithful in the use of whatever we have received. Then, if God chooses to entrust more to us, our responsibility ratchets up accordingly.

What assets have been placed under your control?

EVALUATING STEWARDSHIP

Every day, we hear such comments as, "I've worked hard for it," "I've earned it—I deserve it," or "It's my time and I'll do what I want to with it." Yet, in 1 Corinthians 4:7, the apostle Paul asks the believers, "What do you have that you did not receive? And if you did receive it, why do you boast as though you did not?" Whether it is intelligence, physical health and strength, a special aptitude in a specific area of endeavor, or any of a number of other attributes, none of these could have been purchased at your neighborhood grocery store or a Wal-Mart Supercenter. One day, you just realized that you had them. With this in mind, look at the following questions and consider your own thoughts on stewardship. Be willing to discuss your answers with a good friend or in a small group of people who care enough to ask you some tough questions.

1. HAVE YOU EVER ATTENDED A "STEWARDSHIP SUNDAY" AT CHURCH OR PARTICIPATED IN A STEWARDSHIP PROGRAM SPONSORED BY A MINISTRY? IF SO, HOW DID YOU FEEL ABOUT IT?

   Do you resent it when people talk about stewardship, feeling as though they are trying to put you on a guilt trip so that they can convince you to give them some of "your" money? Why? What can churches do to better enlighten and prepare their members about biblical stewardship?

2. WHAT HAS THIS CHAPTER TOLD YOU ABOUT STEWARDSHIP THAT YOU DIDN'T ALREADY KNOW?

   When you think about your personal resources, whether it be your money, your "stuff," your time, or your personal abilities, do you regard yourself the owner or the caretaker? Explain your answer.

3. AFTER READING THIS CHAPTER, HOW WOULD YOU EVALUATE
YOURSELF AS A STEWARD OF GOD'S RESOURCES?

If you think some changes are necessary, what might some of them be? What steps should you take to make these changes happen?

PRAYING *About* STEWARDSHIP

It would be nice if God would just send us a bill stating, "You owe . . ."—and that would tell us what He expects us to do as stewards of His resources. But it doesn't work that way. In fact, you might say that God's answer to the question What do You want? is simply, Everything! Now might be a good time to present this issue to the Lord, asking how you can be a more effective, more fruitful steward of all that He has entrusted to your care. The following prayer can help you get started:

Lord, I have heard the old saying "You can't outgive God," and I believe it. You have already given me and the world more than I could ever dream of giving You. But perhaps there is more You want me to give, or maybe I haven't given You much access to an area of my life. Lord, show me how to be a better steward of the time and talents you have given to me as well as of my financial and material possessions. Help me learn and remember that I am not the "owner" of these resources, that I am just Your caretaker, entrusted with a small portion of Your infinite riches.

Recommended Resources on Stewardship

Habits of the Heart: Individualism and Commitment in American Life, by Robert Neelly Bellah (editor), Richard Madsen, and William M. Sullivan, University of California Press, 1996.

The Human Equation: Building Profits by Putting People First, by Jeffrey Pfeffer, Harvard Business School Press, 1998.

Involvement, Vols. 1 and 2, by John R. W. Stott, Revell, 1984, 1985.

Love and Profit: The Art of Caring Leadership, by James Autry, Avon, 1992.

The Soul of a Business: Managing for Profit and the Common Good, by Tom Chappell, Bantam Books, 1994.

Stewardship: Choosing Self-Service Over Self-Interest, by Peter Block, Berrett-Koehler, 1993.

The Partnering Puzzle—
Two Are Better Than One

Barbara had invested countless hours to build up her antique business, and the work had paid off. Her shop had attracted a steady clientele and had even merited a feature story in the city's morning newspaper. The question was, where should she go from here? A prime location had just opened up in the mall, but the rent would be more than double what she was currently paying. Could she manage the additional overhead? And Colleen, her longtime friend from college, had offered to invest in the business and had become a partner. Colleen did have better organizational and financial skills, so that would be a definite asset.

Since she had never had a partner before, Barbara wanted to proceed cautiously. The Bible, she remembered, said something about not becoming "unequally yoked with nonbelievers," but she didn't see that as a problem. Colleen was active in her church and was a member of the choir, and she even led one of the women's weeknight Bible studies. So finally, after being approached once more by Colleen, Barbara agreed that they would form a partnership, and she called her attorney to have the papers drawn up.

At first, Barbara thought the arrangement seemed perfect. Colleen did bring strengths in areas where she had felt inadequate. But then she started to see another side of her friend. Colleen had some very strong opinions about what merchandise they should buy and was very unyielding. At the same time, she could be very impulsive. She insisted on going out on a limb to secure a large portion of Mrs. Lawson's estate, even though the purchase would require taking out a huge loan—at least from Barbara's perspective. And Colleen's recent choice of salespeople had been very questionable as well.

"This isn't at all what I expected," Barbara admitted to her husband. "When I got those partnership contracts, why didn't it have 'Beware: Proceed with caution' printed in bold on the front page?"

■ ■

If you mention the name Wilbur, you're not likely to get much reaction. It's not very common these days. The same goes for the name Orville. However, if you talk about Wilbur and Orville, that's a different story. The two names together kindle something in our collective imagination. We can almost see the adventurous Wright brothers tinkering and dreaming in their shop, defying the skeptics, until the day they astonished the world by doing what no one else thought possible: flying through the air, like birds.

Wilbur and Orville first referred to themselves as "The Wright Brothers" when they started their own printing company at ages twenty-two and eighteen, respectively. From then on, they were a pair, collaborating in business and caring for each other in life. In fact, Wilbur was nursing his typhoid-stricken brother when he came across a news item about the death of a famous German glider pilot. It sparked his curiosity and started the brothers down a road that eventually led them to write the first chapter in aviation history.

Throughout their lives, Wilbur and Orville Wright's partnership was strong. On the day when they were to test their new flying machine in Kitty Hawk, North Carolina, Wilbur won the coin toss and climbed into the airplane. It stalled on takeoff. At their next effort, on December 17, 1903, it was Orville's turn, and this time he made it into the air. Between them, there was no grasping for control or credit; there was just a back and forth sharing of duties and glory. Biographers tend to refer to the brothers as a unit, rarely making a distinction between the two brothers, in terms of who was responsible for which advancement. For all practical purposes, they were one in ambition and accomplishment.

Compare their lives with that of another figure, who came onto the scene several decades later. If the Wright Brothers wrote the first chapter of aviation history, Howard Hughes, born three years after that legendary flight from Kitty Hawk, wanted to top the best-seller list and own the screenplay rights. Although he was influential in aviation, defense, electronics, communications, and film, Hughes is probably most remembered for his colossal obsession with power and his unwillingness to share control of any enterprise.

Consider the *Spruce Goose,* one of Hughes's more memorable undertakings. Contracted to produce a wooden cargo- and troop-carrying plane for the government during World War II, Hughes envisioned a grand and breathtaking vessel, with a wingspan of 320 feet—one and a half times that of a modern-day Boeing 747. However, because of Hughes's continual interference in production, the war ended before the *Spruce Goose* made it into the air. It did fly once—for a mile, and then it sat in a hangar, never to fly again. The airplane became a symbol of Hughes himself: ambitious and powerful, but doomed to failure.

Although Hughes was spectacularly wealthy and made his mark as one of America's boldest entrepreneurs, historians are nearly unanimous in their portrayal of Hughes as someone who was power-hungry, unable to trust, and tormented by unhappiness. "By the time he died[,] in 1976," writes one on-line biographer (www.socalhistory.org), ". . . he had become a mentally ill recluse, wasted in body, incoherent in thought, alone in the world except for his doctors and bodyguards. He had squandered millions and brought famous companies to the financial brink. For much of his time on earth, he seemed larger than life, but his end could not have been sadder."

The lives of the Wright Brothers and Hughes provide fuel for speculation: Would Orville, the tinkerer, have been able to invent the airplane without Wilbur, the brainier and more visionary of the pair? Would Wilbur have been able to put legs to his dream without Orville's mechanical prowess? And what if Hughes had released his death grip on his enterprises and allowed another individual to share the burdens and compensate for his weaknesses? The endings might have been different.

The two stories represent opposite ends of the partnership spectrum—with Orville and Wilbur so closely linked that we're not sure where one man ends and the other begins, and with Howard Hughes so solitary that he would rather fail than share control. Partnership has become a buzzword of sorts in today's business world, with more and more companies recognizing the advantages of alliance. According to Andersen Consulting, corporate alliances will represent up to $40 trillion in value within the next few years. "More and more of us are faced with having to achieve breakthrough goals and to solve complex problems," says Robert Hargrove, in *Mastering the Art of Creative Collaboration* (McGraw-Hill, 1998). In a recent issue of *Fast Company*, he states, "You can't do that alone. The only way to meet these kinds of challenges is through collaboration."

But is partnership only about joining forces for greater profit? That's part of it. But partnering has rewards that go much deeper. True partnership is a relationship that extends beyond commercial transaction, and it is marked by structural overlap and mutual benefit. According to *Getting Partnering Right*, by Neil Rackham, Lawrence Friedman, and Richard Ruff (McGraw-Hill, 1995), a true partnership involves impact, intimacy, and vision—a relationship in which trust and a focus on the greater good are of utmost importance.

The GRIM REALITY *of* AUTONOMY

In some ways, the characteristics of a solitary life can be powerfully seductive. We get to make our own decision, set our own schedule, and be accountable only to ourself. There are no interruptions or distractions. Plus, when we're successful on our own, we can keep all the profits, all the credit, and all the glory.

But Solomon, the writer of Ecclesiastes, paints a dark picture of that kind of life. As he's exploring the subject of meaninglessness in chapters 3 and 4, he comes to a sad situation: a man with abundant material wealth who can't enjoy it because he has no partner to share it with (Ecclesiastes 4:8). He has no child, no brother. "For whom am I toiling?" he asks, and we can almost hear the despair in his voice. It's as if the writer is saying, "Be warned. This is no way to live life."

Then, in contrast, Solomon presents a beautiful picture in Ecclesiastes 4:9–12 that begins, "Two are better than one." Why? Because they have a good return for their work. Because one can help the other up when he falls. Because they can keep each other warm. And because they can come to each other's defense. This passage and other examples in scripture show us that God did not intend for people to live or work solo. That's why He created marriage, family, and community. When He formed Adam, He saw that it wasn't good for man to be alone, so He gave him Eve. Consider David and Jonathan, Paul and Barnabas, Christ and the church. They all richly illustrate the life God intended for us to enjoy—that of relationship. And in the context of work, He created partnership, which is the theme of Ecclesiastes 4:9–12.

Even though we often think of this passage in the context of marriage (how often have you heard it read during wedding ceremonies?), Solomon was not talking about marriage but about work. In fact, work is the theme of the entire Book of Ecclesiastes. For example, chapter 3 states that there's a time and a season for every activity under heaven, and in response, verse 9 asks, "What does the worker gain from his toil?" The writer doesn't say, "What does the family gain from the marriage?" He doesn't ask, "What does the church gain from its pastor?" This passage is relevant to those relationships, but Solomon clearly is focused on work.

It's helpful to examine the larger context of the passage. In Ecclesiastes 3:1–15, the writer contends that God sets the agenda and timing for all of life: "I know that everything God does will endure forever" (3:14). But in Ecclesiastes 3:16–4:16, we see people behaving as if they can do whatever they want, in contrast with God's agenda. For example, he says in 3:16–17 that the wicked do whatever they like, but God sees them and will bring them to judgment. In 3:18–21, the writer says that man, unbelievably, thinks he can do whatever he wants, even though he's going to die, just as a dog dies, and he knows it.

Continuing in Ecclesiastes 4:1, we see people in power oppressing those who have no power. In 4:5–6, a man is lazy and does nothing. In 4:8, we see our productive but lonely worker. In 4:13–16, man can listen to advice or not, whatever he feels like.

But in Ecclesiastes 4:9–12, we find a short parenthetical aside that talks about partnership. Why is that parenthetical statement there? It doesn't really fit with the surrounding text that talks about people setting their own—ultimately meaningless—agendas.

Maybe this is what happened: Solomon was rolling along through his logical progression of thoughts, teaching the young leaders who were his audience, when he came to the lonely worker in chapter 4, verse 8. This sad vignette prompted him to briefly divert to a side road. Maybe he said, "Look, I need a time-out here. I know this is a parenthetical thought that interrupts the flow of what we're talking about, but this issue is too important to leave without comment. Working by yourself is a lonely business." Then he enters into the "two are better than one" passage. He's trying to persuade these young leaders not to go too far in life without seriously addressing the possibilities of community and partnership in their work.

Of course, not everyone is outgoing and highly relational. Life isn't always a giant neighborhood party. Some of us seem to work better by ourselves, and some jobs—writing, designing, or accounting, for example—are much more isolated than others. The people in those professions go into the office, shut the door, and get the work done. But, at the same time, an autonomous life that is consumed by isolation is not the model God intended.

To make his case, in verses 9–12 of the fourth chapter of Ecclesiates, Solomon presents his audience with four advantages of partnership.

Benefits *of* Partnership

1. Partnership leads to greater efficiency and productivity.

"Two are better than one," the writer says, "because they have a good return for their work" (Ecclesiastes 4:9). Notice the choice of words. Solomon doesn't say two are good; he says two are *better.* This means that two people together can accomplish more than twice what one person can accomplish. The result of their work is greater than the sum of its parts.

This statement resonates within today's business community, which is preoccupied with figuring out how to take a fixed investment and get the greatest amount of return. This is true of a team leader who is figuring out whether he should put five people on a project, a manager who is deciding whether to allocate a thousand dollars to a trip, or a strategic planner who is thinking about placing $1 million in a stand-alone business unit. The bottom line is: How do I maximize the return on my investment? If I put X in at the beginning, how do I get X squared, X cubed, or at least X plus 1 at the end?

Ecclesiastes says that that kind of productivity and efficiency happens through partnership. But the mere fact that two people say that they are creating a partnership—by starting a business or a church together, for example—does not mean that the benefits are automatically theirs. Let's say that an accountant's "partner" is her calculator. The calculator allows the accountant to be much more effective in her work. But she can't just go buy a calculator, set it on her desk, and expect to become more productive. She must use it and use it correctly. The same is true with partnership. It must involve a true crossing over of lives for the benefits to follow.

Greater productivity and efficiency are why the words *team* and *partnership* have become such prominent parts of the business vocabulary in the past ten years. Using a partnership concept adds to your bottom line. Each party brings to a relationship something that the other lacks, resulting in a combined team more competitive than its separate parts. That's what Solomon means when he says, "Two are better than one, because they have a good return for their work."

2. PARTNERING ALLOWS YOU TO SHARE RISK AND REWARD.

"If one falls down, his friend can help him up. But pity the man who falls and has no one to help him up" (Ecclesiastes 4:10). With partnership, you get twice the celebration and half the pain. That's a pretty good deal.

If there's one guarantee in life, it's that we're all going to hit some bumpy roads. There will be economic downturns. There will be bad Mondays and even worse Fridays. There will be devastating phone calls and disastrous meetings. Proposals will unravel. The industry will face a crisis. Or maybe we'll face a moral collapse. We can be pushed down or throw ourselves down by our own bad decisions. In our personal lives and in our business lives, we all fall down at some point—often many times.

If you have a partner in your world, that person can say, "Here's my hand; I've got my feet firmly planted. Let me help you up." Elan Susser, president of GoldMine Software Corp. in Pacific Palisades, California, agrees. "You need someone who lifts you up when you're down," he has said of his partner and executive vice president, Jon Ferrara. Consider a solitary runner. When he falls down, he has to get back up and catch up in the race. But what if he were on a team and the instant he fell down, someone else stepped in and ran for a while? Instead of a solo sprint, it would be a relay. A partnership doesn't just help us up for our own sake; it keeps the work going.

The text is not making the case that once you've fallen, you can't get up on your own and you're left to the vultures. The assumption is that people do get up after they fall, but it takes much longer and you lose some rhythm when you have to get up by yourself—which is another reason why "two are better than one."

If partnership's helping hand allows us to cut our risk in half, it also doubles our reward. Success is much sweeter when there's someone to celebrate it with, because it doesn't happen in a vacuum.

3. PARTNERSHIP CREATES INNOVATION, BREAKTHROUGH, AND DISCOVERY.

"If two lie down together, they will keep warm. But how can one keep warm alone?" (Ecclesiastes 4:11). On a cold night outside, a blanket by itself isn't much help. It might trap a little body heat, but to really get warm you need another body to generate warmth. When Boy Scouts go to sleep in their sleeping bags, they'll start the night evenly spread over the tent floor. But if the temperature drops, more likely than not, they'll be huddled in clusters by morning, each boy subconsciously seeking the warmth of his friends during the chilly night.

Or take hypothermia victims. If someone's health has been so compromised by extreme cold that he can no longer regulate his own body temperature, survival experts say to take off the person's clothes, put him in a sleeping bag, and put another person in the sleeping bag with him. The hypothermia sufferer will draw heat from the healthy person's body and will soon be out of danger. The key ingredient in the formula is the other person's warmth.

The same is true in a business context, where heat can be thought of as innovation. Consider a brainstorming meeting. One person can't come up with all the possible good ideas on his or her own; it takes intense collaboration. One person's comment sparks a thought from the other, and that helps the first person see a new possibility that neither had considered. They experience the genesis of something new, different, and exciting that no one person could have come up with alone. The solution came from the combination of brains together.

Traditionally, people regard this verse to be about comfort. Certainly, warmth is comfortable, but it's also a catalyst for change. How do you make fire? By rubbing one stick against another. You can't set one stick on top of a rock and say, "Go, fire, go!" It works only if there are two.

4. PARTNERSHIP PROVIDES SAFETY, DEFENSE, AND STRENGTH.

When the United States sends troops into a volatile area for a peacekeeping mission, the Marines are often the first to go. When they arrive, they climb down ropes out of helicopters two by two, and then they hit the ground and stand back to back. Two Marines back to back have a 360-degree perspective. This is what the writer of Ecclesiastes is saying: "Though one may be overpowered, two can defend themselves. A cord of three strands is not quickly broken" (Ecclesiastes 4:12).

A person standing alone can, at best, see only 180 degrees. That leaves a lot of ground unguarded and vulnerable to attack. But a partner can cover that area. Say an employee wants a job promotion and puts only his or her best side on display, or another business wants to make a deal with you. A partner can protect you from being taken advantage of; that person sees the 180 degrees that you don't see.

When two partners stand back to back, they are so closely connected that an attack on one is an attack on the other. They're woven together, like a rope that is stronger than any individual strand. In the workplace, if you're looking to grow, you may need one or two partners before you'll have the strength to do so. Or, if someone misunderstands your motives or actions, a partner can provide safety and protection by advocating your position.

A partner also protects us when we need to spend time with our family or a personal crisis takes us away from work. The partner is there to pick up and carry on. Partners protect each other's time and energy, and they protect each other from making bad decisions legally, organizationally, or financially. No one, no matter how talented, has all the bases covered, and it's those weaker areas where we're vulnerable. A partner will protect us from ourself.

TRUTHS *About* PARTNERSHIP

As the writer of Ecclesiastes lists the benefits of partnership, an interesting progression takes place. The first benefit is relatively impersonal: let's do something together so that we can have a good return. The second benefit is a bit more personal: let me help you up. The third benefit represents a great leap in personal involvement: you don't get under a blanket with someone without thinking twice. With the fourth benefit, which uses the rope illustration, there is no longer a recognition of individuality; the strands are woven together into a unit. This progression shows us that partnerships are not static; they change and develop along with the relationship.

In thinking about the benefits of partnership, there are some summary statements that we should keep in mind:

- God's model for engaging and enjoying life to its fullest involves community. We don't do family, church, or work by ourselves—at least not very much; there's very little that we do solo. The writer of Ecclesiastes is extending the idea of community by talking about partnership, which is one facet of life in community.

- Partnering is one model of community that we can all can participate in, no matter where we work. We don't have to quit our job and be entrepreneurial. A partner might be a certain vendor with whom our department already has a strong relationship or it might be a coworker whose personality and goals are in line with ours.

- Partnering doesn't automatically mean that we will never fall down or that we will never get cold. Partnership doesn't let us circumvent the difficulties of our work, but it does give us another person to face them with.

- The benefits associated with the next level of partnership happen only when the partners are committed to attaining that next level. There is a cause-and-effect relationship in partnership that relies on a commitment to change and growth.

- The benefits of partnership far outweigh the complexity. The biggest resistance to partnership is its complexity—scheduling with two or more calendars, dividing responsibilities, and establishing decision-making protocols, for example. And the greatest illusion about a solo life is its seeming simplicity.

- We can't partner with many people at the same time. The writer of Ecclesiastes goes from "two are better than one" to "a cord of three strands," not twenty strands. Partnership involves time, risk, and vulnerability, and to find someone with the right personality, synergy, chemistry, and skill to work with is not an easy task. It won't happen automatically with everyone in our business world.

In short, partnership is an intentional way of life that involves serious investment but rich reward. Solomon is said to have written Ecclesiastes near the end of his life, in the twilight of a reign marked by spectacular material and political success but tainted by moral and spiritual failure. He had hundreds of wives and concubines and many dealings with other ancient rulers, but did he have one person he could call a true partner? Perhaps he recognized the richness of partnership by its absence in his own life. We don't know that. But we do know that he urged us not to live our live alone, not to toil with no one at our side. A partner can make all the difference.

A SPECIAL WORD *About* PARTNERSHIPS

Because partnering of one kind or another—formal, informal, legally binding, or a "gentleman's agreement"—is such a vital part of today's business world, we want to share some additional thoughts on the whole area of partnerships. We hope you will find this special addendum beneficial.

Reflect on your growing-up years and you will likely discover that you began practicing the concept of partnering at a very young age. At a swimming pool, you may have been encouraged to use the buddy system, to always have a partner close by who could help you or call for assistance if you began to struggle in the water. If you participated in the three-legged race on field day, you didn't do it alone but were instead attached to a partner who ran with you. In junior high and high school science classes, you probably had a lab partner who dissected frogs and performed experiments with you.

Such associations formed the basis for the beliefs about partnership that carried you into adulthood. If your experiences were positive, you discovered that partners provided safety and protection. You learned about synergy (although you probably didn't call it that). You found that if you teamed up with a partner who was stronger, smarter, or faster than you, you would place higher in the race or you would get better grades than if you were by yourself.

But if your experience with others was negative, then you may have decided that you would rather work by yourself than be part of a team. You may have found that partners just brought you down and made you carry more than your share of the load, and so you decided that if that was what partnership was all about, you didn't need it.

However, a preference for working by oneself—for whatever reason, as opposed to working in a partnership—fails to take into account what success is all about. Now, the *Merriam-Webster College Dictionary* describes partnership as a "legal relation existing between two or more persons contractually associated as joint principals in a business." But, while that's a good start, we thought the definition should be much broader and deeper than that. We view it this way:

A partnership is an intentional arrangement between individuals or entities that extends beyond mere commercial transaction and is characterized by structural overlap and mutual benefit.

1. A PARTNERSHIP IS AN INTENTIONAL ARRANGEMENT *between individuals or entities.*

As we developed our definition, we wanted to include the concept of partnering in the corporate arena, not just between or among individuals. The intentional relationship previously described can exist between two people who team up to run a company or do projects together, but it can also exist between corporations and nonprofit organizations whose business or ministry interests are intertwined.

2. A PARTNERSHIP IS AN INTENTIONAL ARRANGEMENT BETWEEN INDIVIDUALS OR ENTITIES THAT *extends beyond mere commercial transaction.*

From a corporate standpoint, when two companies have a relationship in which one firm simply buys goods or services from the other, their relationship doesn't qualify as a partnership according to our definition. That is because their affiliation doesn't extend beyond the level of commercial transaction. If the two organizations moved beyond mere buying and selling and began to work together on strategic issues, however, they would begin to fit our definition. Such a partnership could involve linking systems and the sharing of information about sales predictions, consumer trends, infrastructure, marketing, logistics, and so forth.

The same principle applies to individuals. Many people team up as "partners" simply for the financial benefit that results; they can make more money working with someone than they can alone. But a working relationship characterized primarily by commercial transaction is not a partnership; it's a financial arrangement. We believe that a true partnership certainly involves money, but it also encompasses relational aspects such as accountability, assistance, friendship, support, and protection.

3. A PARTNERSHIP IS AN INTENTIONAL ARRANGEMENT BETWEEN
    INDIVIDUALS OR ENTITIES THAT EXTENDS BEYOND MERE
    COMMERCIAL TRANSACTION AND IS *characterized by structural
    overlap*.

By structural overlap, we mean that an individual's work life or an organization's work life is structurally different as a result of the partnership. In other words, the worlds of the individuals or entities involved in the partnership do more than simply touch. Two companies do more than buy and sell from each other. Built into their contractual arrangement is the need to interact, to share confidential information, and to assist each other. Two individual partners do more than share an office space; they sign documents together, they borrow money together, and they own a business together. Such structural overlap can affect income flow, time management decisions, and strategic opportunities.

So how do you know if you have structural overlap? That's fairly easy to answer. If it exists, it is difficult to unravel. But if two people who decide to end their "partnership" can simply go their separate ways, they probably didn't have a structural overlap in the first place.

4. A PARTNERSHIP IS AN INTENTIONAL ARRANGEMENT BETWEEN
    INDIVIDUALS OR ENTITIES THAT EXTENDS BEYOND MERE
    COMMERCIAL TRANSACTION AND IS CHARACTERIZED BY
    STRUCTURAL OVERLAP AND *mutual benefit*.

This part of our definition might be quite obvious, but a partnership needs to be good for everybody. If two companies begin a partnership because they want to have a better working relationship but neither sees a discernible advantage from such an arrangement, the partnership will dissolve quickly. That's because neither will be willing to put forth the effort necessary to take the relationship to the next level. Both parties must be making continual deposits into the business and relationship for it to be a true partnership. If one is always making deposits—providing financial support, coming up with innovative ideas, working late, and so forth, while the other is always making withdrawals—spending the money, never offering creative input, going home early, and so forth, the arrangement is not mutually beneficial.

The ownership structure doesn't have to be fifty-fifty. It doesn't have to be exactly equal. But there has to be parity. A partnership is not a mentor-protégé or teacher-student type of relationship. It's a peer-to-peer affiliation. If a mentor and protégé decide to become partners and they have not or cannot transition into a peer-to-peer situation, the protégé will almost always feel patronized and the mentor will almost always feel unfairly burdened by all the work that needs to be done. That is not what mutual benefit is all about.

Evaluating Partnering

A businessman once announced at a local Chamber of Commerce meeting, "I'm a self-made man," to which one of his counterparts commented, "Oh, well that explains it!" There can be a certain pride in being able to declare, "I did it myself," but realistically, in most cases we can accomplish far more if we work with others. The analogy of the two workhorses that together can pull many times more than they could independently applies to business and professional life. Let the questions that follow help you make an appraisal as to how well you partner with others. Be sure to discuss your thoughts candidly with at least one other person.

1. What is your working style? Are you a loner, tending to do things by yourself, or do you prefer to work with others?
    Why do you think you prefer to work the way you do? Is it just your natural bent, or was it something you learned from someone else—a parent, a friend, or someone in the workplace? If you are work-

ing alone, are there ways in which you think you could become more productive if you partnered with others?

2. *Teamwork* SEEMS TO BE A POPULAR BUZZWORD IN BUSINESS CIRCLES THESE DAYS, BUT CAN YOU THINK OF EXAMPLES OF WORKING GROUPS THAT ARE TRULY FUNCTIONING EFFECTIVELY AS A TEAM?

   Do any so-called teams come to your mind that in reality are little more than a collection of individuals with little conception of harmony or synergy? What do you think are some of the obstacles to effective teamwork?

3. IN 2 CORINTHIANS 6:14, WE ARE WARNED AGAINST BECOMING "UNEQUALLY YOKED WITH UNBELIEVERS." HOW DOES THIS RELATE TO THE CONTEMPORARY WORKPLACE? DOES THIS MEAN THAT FOLLOWERS OF CHRIST SHOULD NOT WORK CLOSELY WITH THOSE WHO HAVE NOT PLACED THEIR FAITH IN HIM?

   If you were considering a formal, legal partnership with someone—perhaps in starting a new business, how would the preceding verse influence your decision?

PRAYING *About* PARTNERING

It's clear that God feels that we can accomplish far more together than we can apart, and He calls us to team up to advance His purposes. But do you feel the same way? Does your approach to your work, as well as to other endeavors, reflect this conviction? Consider the following prayer as you appraise your own attitude toward partnering with others in various endeavors.

God, my desire is to become all that You want me to be, but I realize that I will need the help and support of others to accomplish that. If there are areas in which I am failing to effectively partner with my peers— blind spots—please enable me to recognize that and make necessary changes. And if pride is inhibiting me from becoming an effective team member because I would rather get all the credit than share it, forgive me and enable me to realize that in Your eyes the whole is truly greater than the sum of the parts.

Recommended Resources on Partnering

Eisenhower and Churchill: The Partnership That Saved the World, by James C. Humes, Prima Publishing, 2001.

Getting Partnering Right: How Market Leaders Are Creating Long-Term Competitive Advantage, by Neil Rackham, Lawrence Friedman, and Richard Ruff, McGraw-Hill Professional Publishing, 1995.

Smart Things to Know About Partnerships, by John L. Mariotti, Capstone Publishing, 2002.

The Strategic Partnering Handbook: The Practitioners' Guide to Partnerships and Alliances, by Tony Lendrum, McGraw-Hill Professional Publishing, 2001.

An Exceptional Calling—
With No Exceptions

Joanne was good at her work. In fact, she was by far the best financial planner in her company. Her expertise, coupled with her sincere interest in and concern for her clients, not only resulted in acquiring and retaining a lot of lucrative contracts but also gave her a never-ending stream of new referrals. Her knowledge of investment strategies and professionalism—coupled with a compassionate, client-centered philosophy of doing business—put her in high demand. While some of her counterparts regularly scrambled to find prospects, Joanne often had to turn away potential clients, because she didn't have the time to give them the attention they deserved.

Yet down deep, she felt dissatisfied and unfulfilled. "Yes, I enjoy my work, I admit that," she explained to a friend over lunch, "but somehow I feel like I have missed my calling. I faithfully attend church, and I try to serve God in a variety of ways, but it seems like my work always gets in the way."

In her mind, people who were "called"—those who were really committed to serving the Lord—found themselves on a mission field in some distant land, working in a vocational capacity for a church or denomination, or they were dedicating their skills and experience to some parachurch ministry that had carved out a specific segment of society that needed to see and hear about the Good News of Jesus Christ and how they could participate in it.

"What I wouldn't do to be able to go full-time for God!" Joanne finally blurted out.

Across the table, without blinking, her friend responded, "What makes you think you haven't already done that?"

Joanne blinked and then asked, with a look of utter surprise, "What do you mean?"

"Well, it seems to me that you are doing a darn good job of serving God as a financial planner. In fact, you are the best I know, and you demonstrate excellence every day! Yes, you have a number of very well-off clients, and you get a very nice income from working with them. But you don't restrict yourself to people with large bank accounts. I know that you readily help confused widows figure out what they should do. You offer free advice to young mothers who are struggling to stretch their meager income to meet their children's needs. And I know of several couples you have counseled who have been able to avoid bankruptcy by finally learning how to handle their finances just by following biblical principles."

A tear gathered in the corner of one of Joanne's eyes as the sense of what her friend was saying settled in, but, fearful that her emotion might come pouring out, she remained silent.

■ ■

All followers of Jesus are called. Individually. In regard to their work.

We were created by Jesus Christ to do something eternally significant at work. When we listen for the voice of Jesus and obey His call to a personal work assignment, we become part of fulfilling God's purpose and agenda in the world.

But hearing and responding to His voice isn't always a simple process.

We have a friend who loves to fish. Every year, he goes on a fishing expedition with three friends. Three of those annual trips have been on the Buffalo River in the Ozark National Forest, here in Arkansas. The last twenty-five miles of the Buffalo River, just before it dumps into the White River, is a remote wilderness area with no road access. Besides having breathtaking beauty, it is peaceful and serene, and you almost never see any other people there.

It takes four days of floating and camping to fish all the way to the White River. You haven't really lived until you've done a little top-water smallmouth bass fishing on the lower end of the Buffalo.

But the group's first trip was memorable for more than just the fishing. As usual, the trip was equipment heavy. They loaded all their food and camping and fishing gear into the flat-bottomed, eighteen-foot riverboats. They waved good-bye to the stranger who had promised to deliver the cars to them at the end of the trip. And then they shoved off and went on their way.

In less than four hundred yards into the twenty-five-mile trip, there is a sharp bend to the right. As they approached the turn, they heard a noise that sounded distinctly like a waterfall. Directly ahead was a steep drop. They couldn't believe it. They had been in the water for less than five minutes, their cars were gone, and no one expected to see them for four days.

They were not happy. There were some mumbled comments like, "I thought this was supposed to be the Buffalo, not Niagara." Then, they huddled up and did all that they knew to do. They got into the water and wrestled the boats, one by one, around the drop-off and through the rapids. In order to have four wonderful days of fishing, they had to do some tricky navigation at the beginning of the trip.

Understanding the calling of Jesus on our work life often feels like trying to pilot a fragile boat through troubled waters. It can be an unsettling process. Hard questions have to be asked, like, What was I created to accomplish? Am I fulfilled through the work I am doing? Is this the work Jesus wants me to do? Am I continually pulled in other directions and toward other opportunities?

Sometimes, career course corrections and transitions are the result. But the earlier we hear and heed the calling of Jesus in regard to our career, the more productive and meaningful our life at work will be.

What is a *calling*? What does it mean to be called by Jesus to our work?

1. WE ARE CALLED BY JESUS TO SERVE GOD'S PURPOSE.

Calling is Jesus Christ's personal invitation for us to work on His agenda, using the talents we've been given, in ways that are eternally significant. The invitation from Jesus is personal to each individual.

Our work involves God's agenda in history. Jesus created us with a gift-mix and an internal wiring package that aligns with our work assignment. And the work He calls us to has eternal significance. What could possibly be more fulfilling?

The concept of calling in scripture is confusing if we don't understand the difference between calling, purpose, and meaning. They are not the same, but they are closely connected.

Purpose in scripture is synonymous with God's sovereign design, His overarching view of history, and what He is accomplishing. We are to serve God's purpose, whatever it is, even though we do not necessarily know all the details.

For example, Acts 1:36 points out that King David "served God's purpose in his own generation." David's work included stints as a shepherd, a musician, a soldier, and a king. Did David know how the work he was called to do fit into God's agenda for history? Yes, to some degree. How? Because God gave David an explanation that is recorded in 2 Samuel 7:5–16. Are most followers of Jesus aware of how their work contributes to God's agenda in history? No. Access to that kind of detailed background information regarding God's purpose is very unusual, even for the men and women we meet in the pages of scripture. We may or may not know God's purpose. But we *must* know and understand God's call. That is our job.

Many people think that their purpose will be fulfilled if they make it to the next rung on the ladder or when they become their own boss, launching their own company. They are pulled to do something bigger, but that search for purpose is always outside their grasp. However, to search for purpose in career advancements, in our increasing net worth, or in fulfilling our dreams completely misses the point. These are not the things that give our work purpose. Our work has purpose because a called work effort contributes to God's agenda for this place and this time. Put differently, our work has eternal significance when we are called to what we are doing. We serve God's purpose by listening for, knowing, and obeying the calling of Jesus Christ on our work life.

If we serve God's purpose by knowing our calling, work satisfaction then comes as a gift from Him. Near the end of his life, King Solomon wrote the book of Ecclesiastes. In it, he hammered at the theme that a godly man will find meaning, satisfaction, and fulfillment in his work: "A man can do nothing better than to eat and drink and find satisfaction in his work. This too, I see, is from the hand of God, for without Him, who can eat or find enjoyment?" (Ecclesiastes 2:24–25).

Solomon repeats the same encouragement in Ecclesiastes 3:12–13, 3:22, and 5:18. But his answer to the question Does everyone receive the gift of work satisfaction from God? is no; only those who are followers of Jesus receive this gift. He states, "To the man who pleases Him, God gives wisdom, knowledge and happiness, but to the sinner he gives the task of gathering and storing up wealth to hand it over to the one who pleases God" (Ecclesiastes 2:26).

We serve God's purpose by knowing God's calling. Then God offers us the gift of work satisfaction.

2.   OUR CALLING IS WORK-SPECIFIC.

Calling in the Bible refers to Jesus calling us to Himself, as well as Jesus calling us to a specific work assignment. When the apostle Paul proclaims (in Romans 8:28, KJV) that we are "called according to His purpose," he is explaining how Jesus saves us and adopts us into His family. But when God says to Jeremiah, "Before you were born . . . I appointed you as a prophet to the nations" (Jeremiah 1:5), the calling is to a specific *work* assignment. God had a job for Jeremiah.

God also had work for Moses; his instructions to him were very specific: "I am sending you to Pharaoh," God says, "to bring my people the Israelites out of Egypt" (Exodus 3:10). That work assignment was to occupy Moses for the rest of his career and life, a span of more than forty years.

God's call to work is woven as a theme from Genesis to Revelation—including Abraham in Genesis 12:1, Joshua in Numbers 27:18–23, Deborah in Judges 4, Nehemiah in Nehemiah 1, and Matthew in Mark 2:14. The list goes on and on, and it presents a clear picture: God calls people to work.

God has work for each of us. Our job is not some arbitrary and random choice that makes no difference. Its primary objective is not to put food on the table and provide a comfortable retirement. It is not some unfortunate necessity so that we may enjoy the "fun stuff," such as vacations, weekends, and retirement. Work is not a punishment or a curse. Our individual work calling is part of God's larger agenda in history. To be called to our work means that we know that what we are doing is what Jesus wants us to do—and what He has designed us to do. This should allow us to bring a tremendous energy and enthusiasm to our work.

But we also need to be careful. Work is not the sum total of our life, nor was it ever meant to be. We must never hide behind our calling as an excuse for our work to own us in inappropriate ways. As one who is called, we will work very hard. But it is Jesus who calls us, not our job. Unless we understand that distinction, the job that Jesus calls us to can actually end up calling us away from Him.

3.   JESUS DESIGNED US SPECIFICALLY FOR OUR WORK ASSIGNMENT.

The people in most organizations approach work in very different ways. They do similar tasks. They share the same values. They use the same technology. But they are very different.

For example, engineers operate best when a process is in place or can be designed. They love systems. They say things like, "A good process turns out a good product." Their thinking is linear. Knowing and following procedure is important. In their way of thinking, the best work is done behind the scenes, in preparation for rolling it out to the public.

Other professionals are in their best element as facilitators in a fast-moving meeting full of complex problems and difficult issues. They revel in the free flow of information and ideas. Put them into a pressure situation where they have to think on their feet and figure things out on the spot, and they will shine. In their way of thinking, the best work is done in public. Behind-the-scenes preparation is okay, but it may not prove to be that relevant.

Each of us was designed from the very beginning by God to accomplish His purpose. Listen to David reflect on the wonder of how God uniquely shapes us for our work assignments:

For you created my inmost being;
*   you knit me together in my mother's womb.*
I praise you because I am fearfully
and wonderfully made;
*   your works are wonderful,*
*   I know that full well.*
My frame was not hidden from you

when I was made in the secret place.
When I was woven together in the depths of the earth,
your eyes saw my unformed body.
All the days ordained for me
were written in your book
before one of them came to be (Psalm 139).

Each of us was designed from the very beginning by God to accomplish His purpose. Would it make any sense for God to form and equip us with precise intention, and then call us to do something that does not fit who we are? If God created us to serve His purpose, and if God formed and "wired" us with awesomely precise intention, then our calling should be closely aligned with our makeup.

Jesus is calling. Are we listening? Have we heard? Are we doing what He has asked of us?

MYTHS *of* CALLING

Before we leave this discussion of the biblical concept of calling, we need to be clear not only about what calling *is* but also about what it *is not*. To accurately understand how God works and what He expects of us, we need to be able to distinguish what we believe to be truth from what actually *is* the truth. To believe incorrectly amounts to trusting in a myth, and holding to a myth is close to believing a lie.

How people come to believe in myths is a topic worthy of research by social scientists. But until they enlighten us, we are left with this fact: we believe and perpetuate myths every day of our life. Consider these natural myths that many people would swear are true:

- Once a fish is caught, it won't ever bite again.
- Lightning won't hit the same tree twice.
- Snakes can't strike while they're in the water.
- Snapping turtles won't let go until it thunders.

Now, consider this list of commonly held myths connected to the concept of calling:

MYTH 1: GOD ONLY *calls* PEOPLE TO GO UP THE LADDER.

We seem always to hear of a colleague who has been *called* to take the "promotion" with a raise, a new title, and a corner office. Or it's the pastor responding to God's call to "move up" to the bigger, better church. Or it's the testimony of the coach who feels God leading him "up" to the Division I football program.

Yes, the cream rises to the top. But that might be more a matter of life and business theory than the way God is orchestrating His people. Did the twelve disciples think they were moving up when Jesus called them to their new work assignment? Did Abraham feel that he was moving up when God called him to leave Ur—the New York, London, or Paris of his day—and live out of a tent? It seems that God calls us not just up, but also over, around, through—and even down—at times.

MYTH 2: GOD SOMETIMES CALLS US TO DO SOMETHING THAT IS
IMMORAL OR DESTRUCTIVE.

This is a particularly popular myth among those who need to justify their self-serving actions. For instance, there was the guy who said, "God has called me to divorce my wife, leave my children, and start a new life on the beach." Another guy really felt that God was leading him to play the lottery (with 50 percent of his paycheck every week), because he "knew" he would win and could give some back to his church. God will not guide against Himself! If we hear "the call" to steal a little money from the petty cash drawer, to leverage a friendship for a deal, or to take a job that will destroy our family, it's not God on the phone—it's someone else calling, and we would be wise not to answer.

MYTH 3: GOD WILL NOT CALL US BECAUSE OF SOME SIN OR FAILURE
IN OUR PAST.

Without a doubt, skeletons in the closet make life more difficult. And some failures disqualify us from some work assignments. But as a general rule, God does not erase our name and number from His Rolodex when we fail. If God did not use cracked pots and broken branches to build His kingdom, everyone would be out of work.

MYTH 4: GOD ONLY CALLS PEOPLE TO JOBS THAT ARE SPECTACULAR
AND BEAUTIFUL.

Everyone can't be at the top of the food chain. Personal ambition—
an overachiever muscle or deep-seated personal insecurities—might
make us think that we are destined for greatness when that is not
God's plan.

Every part of preparing for a concert is critical. For a concert to
take place, the building must be scheduled and people must prepare
the facilities, check the equipment, sell the tickets, manage the crowd,
park the cars, sell the snacks, and plug in the lights, and musicians
must practice for the concert.

MYTH 5: CALLING IS SUPPOSED TO BE A CONFUSING AND
MYSTERIOUS EVENT.

It's time to connect a few dots. First, God is not confused or unclear
about what He thinks. Second, God is a communicator by His very
nature. He has taken the initiative to communicate with humankind
from the very beginning. These two truths should dispel the myth that
God's calling is supposed to be a stumble through the fog. If we are
confused, perhaps we aren't listening for God's voice. Just because we
don't hear doesn't mean He is not calling.

MYTH 6: CALLING CAN'T HAPPEN WHEN YOU ARE YOUNG.

Don't tell this to the Old Testament prophet Jeremiah or young Timothy in the New Testament. And don't interview Daniel, the thor-
oughbred Chief Creative Officer of four political administrations in
ancient Babylon. As a matter of fact, many people testify that the
younger years are less restrained, making it actually easier to discover
personal calling.

MYTH 7: CALLING CAN'T HAPPEN WHEN YOU ARE OLD.

It's not an age thing. It's a communication thing. God doesn't stop
having purpose when our knees go weak, our vision gets blurred, or
our hair turns gray (or turns loose). We are never too old to incorpo-
rate purpose and intention into our life, including our work life. Many
people are experiencing a fresh sense of calling when they reach fifty,
sixty, seventy, and beyond. They are on the backside of a first work

assignment, and God calls them to a new task. They might move to more of a mentoring role in their existing job or they might change their career altogether. But it's not retirement, it's reassignment.

MYTH 8: IF YOU DON'T BELIEVE IN JESUS, CALLING HAS NO IMPACT ON YOUR LIFE.

Max works in a large, publicly held company. His boss, Jack, is not a follower of Jesus and neither are most of the people who work with Max. Through a dialogue with a friend, Max began to better understand his specific calling to that work assignment. The results were astounding! He takes more initiative in his job, and he even has done some extra training to get better at his task. He no longer daydreams about another job, a different company, and so forth. He shows up with purpose in his eyes, enthusiasm in his step, loyalty in his language, and personal ownership in his actions.

His boss gave him the best annual review in his twelve-year tenure. It opened with this question: "Max, what has happened to you?" Max answered, "I discovered my calling."

His boss didn't have a calling and probably didn't understand why it was important to Max. Nevertheless, when Max began to live out his calling, it had an impact on everyone around him.

MYTH 9: CALLING ALWAYS MEANS MOVING FROM SECULAR WORK TO SPIRITUAL WORK.

For some people, this statement is true; it's not true for everybody. Dean and Don were both pastors in southern California. Through a series of events, they both began to sense that God was calling them into business. They responded, teamed up, and launched out into the business world. Did they throw away their communication gifts? No. They simply extended them toward their specific calling. And, today, DaySpring Greeting Cards is one of the largest greeting card companies in the world. God moves people in both directions.

MYTH 10: GOD'S CALL ONLY CONCERNS SALVATION.

Some people believe that God does not get involved in the details of their jobs. To believe this cuts against the idea that we are individually and uniquely created by God. And it rejects the notion that God left His artist's touch on each of us—His fingerprints on the unique gift-mix that we each possess. We each have certain motivated abilities and talents that are uniquely shaped to be expressed in our life and work, not just in our salvation.

MYTH 11: CALLING IS ONLY A MASCULINE ACTIVITY.

This misconception probably comes from the belief of some people that calling is what God does to secure more pastors and missionaries when there's a shortage, and that only men are intended to fill such roles, which some people consider masculine work. But nowhere does scripture teach this, and nowhere does life prove this to be true. Men and women alike have been apportioned gifts and talents for use in life and work—including work as pastors and missionaries.

MYTH 12: NOT ALL WORK ASSIGNMENTS CARRY A CALLING.

Actually, this is part truth, part myth. God will not call someone to be a bank robber, an assassin, a town drunk, or a drug smuggler. But everyone can experience God's individual work assignment calling. That applies to the banker and the builder, the dentist and the apprentice, the politician and the statistician, the preacher and the teacher, the salesman and the surgeon, the farmer and the broker, the machinist and the artist.

MYTH 13: BEING CALLED TO A WORK ASSIGNMENT AUTOMATICALLY
RESULTS IN MOTIVATION, PEACE, FULFILLMENT, AND
CONTENTMENT.

Every job has its rough edges. Even those of us who believe that we are squarely in the center of the optimal job fit will experience a few days of cloudiness, demotivation, boredom, and, perhaps, burnout. Being called to a job assignment doesn't shield us from the normal rhythms of work. It doesn't guarantee that we will not be overlooked for a position. It doesn't mean that we will happily whistle our way to work every Monday morning. And it doesn't mean that we won't drag ourself into our driveway some Friday afternoons and mumble, "There's gotta be a better job than this."

Calling is not the magic silver bullet that makes all the struggles connected with work disappear. But, clearly, those of us who are experiencing a deep sense of calling in our work life should indicate

more motivation, more peace, more fulfillment, and more contentment than those who aren't.

Some myths don't cause much injury, even though they are
wrong. So what if we believe that snapping turtles don't let go until it
thunders? However, not all ignorance turns out to be harmless bliss.
Believing myths about calling can mean misunderstanding the voice
of Jesus in our work life. These "snakes" really do strike while they are
in the water.

EVALUATING CALLING

Through the centuries, believers have struggled to discern what the
calling of God was, how it could be found, and how one could be certain of it as he or she proceeded into the future. "I wish He would just
write it on the wall so that it would be clear and I wouldn't have to
wonder about it," more than one person has said with some exasper-
ation. Yet, as we have seen in this chapter, God's calling is not some
mysterious, needle-in-the-haystack pursuit. Perhaps you are one of the
minority, feeling confident about your calling; or maybe, like most
people, you often wonder if where you are and what you are doing is
God's best for you and your life. Consider the following questions and,
with a trusted friend or with a small group of people, take an honest
look at your current thinking about God's calling in general and His
calling specifically for your life.

1. HAS THIS CHAPTER CAUSED YOU TO REEVALUATE YOUR
    UNDERSTANDING OF BIBLICAL CALLING?
    If so, what were your ideas of what "calling" meant before you
read this chapter? Have you ever thought that the calling of God always involved work in a full-time, vocational sense?

2. CAN YOU IDENTIFY WITH ANY OF THE MYTHS ABOUT CALLING
    THAT ARE REVIEWED IN THIS CHAPTER?
    How do you think these myths developed? Have you ever heard
them expressed—specifically or by inclination—in your church or in
a gathering of friends who shared your spiritual commitment?

3. IN LIGHT OF WHAT YOU NOW UNDERSTAND FROM THIS CHAPTER,
    AND THE WORK THAT YOU PRESENTLY DO, WOULD YOU SAY THAT
    YOU NOW HAVE A NEW, CLEARER SENSE OF CALLING, OR DO YOU
    STILL BELIEVE THAT ULTIMATELY, PERHAPS SOON, GOD IS CALLING
    YOU TO DO SOMETHING ELSE?

    Explain how you have reached this conclusion and ask a friend,
or a small group of people, to challenge your thinking in this area.

PRAYING *About* CALLING

It would truly be a tragedy to come to the end of one's life and realize
that God's calling had been missed or squandered. But wouldn't it be
equally tragic to fail to recognize that the Lord had called you to serve
Him—and others—right where you are, at least for the present? Perhaps the following prayer will help you express your thoughts and understanding of God's calling for you:

> *Lord, in the Scriptures, You do not distinguish between secular and*
> *sacred work. In the Old Testament, Daniel and Joseph did not hold spiri-*
> *tual jobs, yet they served Your people in incredible ways. And Paul writes*
> *that even on his missionary journeys, he still continued to pursue tent mak-*
> *ing as needed. Lord, please enable me to have a clearer understanding and*
> *appreciation of the vocational role You have called me to and, as necessary,*
> *renew my sense of calling as I carry out my responsibilities on Monday*
> *morning—or Thursday afternoon. Give me a sense of the supernatural in*
> *the middle of the mundane.*

Recommended Resources on Calling

Business as a Calling: Work and the Examined Life, by Michael Novak, Free Press, 1996.
The Call, by Os Guinness, W Publishing Group, 1998.
Finding a Job You Can Love, by Ralph T. Mattson and Arthur F. Miller, P&R Publish-
     ing, 1999.
The Fourth Frontier: Exploring the New World of Work, by Thomas G. Addington and
     Stephen R. Graves, W Publishing Group, 2000.
What Color Is Your Parachute? by Richard Nelson Bolles, Ten Speed Press, 2001.

10

Why Rest When There's So Much to Do?

Friends often called Fred a workaholic, but it never bothered him. In fact, he considered the term a compliment, a badge of honor. "I come from a family of hard workers," Fred thought to himself. "I never want anyone to accuse me of getting anything that I didn't pour out good sweat to earn." Working six days a week was normal for him, and if a project demanded it, he would leave the worship service on Sunday and drive straight to the office without even pausing for dinner. A vacation? That was something for people without much ambition or motivation.

When his wife begged him to take a week off and enjoy some extended time with the family, Fred dismissed the notion. "If you want to take a few days and go off with your sister and her kids, or one of your friends, I don't have any problem with that. I just have too much to do. Taking vacation time would put me too far behind."

Because he was an avid jogger and avoided common pitfalls such as smoking, eating improperly, and abusing alcohol, Fred managed to maintain his health despite his self-demanding work schedule. However, his lifestyle did take a toll. Dennis, who had worked as Fred's vice president of sales, suffered a massive heart attack. Although he survived, the coronary left him totally disabled. Reflecting back, Fred realized that Dennis had tried to follow his lead, putting in almost identical work hours and demanding almost the same from his sales team.

Just weeks before, Fred's wife had asked, "What's it going to take to get through to you and convince you to slow down?" Looking at Dennis lying in his intensive care bed, Fred shook his head and thought, "No one's going to have to tell him to slow down anymore." Feeling that he should have been the one to be stricken—and feeling in one sense that he had been—Fred finally began to ask himself, "Maybe I should start slowing down and get some rest. But after working so hard and for so long all of these years, do I even know *how* to rest?"

■ ■

We recently had a conversation with a fellow believer, an executive who oversees hundreds of employees. He loves the Lord and knows scripture well. Our dialogue with him came to an abrupt halt when we mentioned the issue of rest. "Rest?!" he said. "I want people to work, not rest. Why would I want them to read about rest?"

Good question. In our world of work, what is rest good for?

To "work" is to perform an action. To "rest" is also to perform an action. Both actions require deliberate focus to succeed. But if history and experience are valid indicators, resting well often demands greater effort than working well.

Resting is difficult. Not because we disdain the concept in theory but because the practical consequence of resting involves not working. It is fruitless to consider rest without measuring its impact on work. "If I rest while others do not," one might reason, "then I could very well lose my place in line, squander opportunities, or give away money. I risk accomplishing less and receiving mediocre recognition. I might look lazy and unconnected to my career. Besides, it seems that the folks who think that rest is a good idea have already made their mark and their money—they can afford to rest." Rest rarely leaves us with any immediate sense of accomplishment. Rest never catalyzes our endorphins.

But even in our superheated economy, where business possibilities abound, rest is suddenly fashionable. "Sleep, that rare commodity in stressed-out America, is the new status symbol," *Wall Street Journal* reporter Nancy Jeffrey has written. "Once derided as a wimpish failing—by the same 1980s overachievers who cried 'Lunch is for Losers' and also believed [that] 'Sleep is for Suckers'—slumber is now being touted as the restorative companion to the creative executive mind."

Netscape cofounder Marc Andreessen, Amazon.com CEO Jeff Bezos, and Snapple creator Michael Weinstein are among the leading chief executives who, according to Jeffrey, reported that they make a habit of getting at least eight hours of sleep each night.

A BIBLICAL IMPERATIVE

Whereas sleep is just now gaining a kind of cultural cachet, rest has always been biblical. Indeed, few topics receive more attention in the Scriptures, and that emphasis begins in the inaugural chapters of Genesis: "By the seventh day God had finished the work He had been doing; so on the seventh day He rested from all His work. And God blessed the seventh day and made it holy, because on it He rested from all the work of creating that He had done" (Genesis 2:2–3).

Biblical rest lies opposite biblical work on the same coin. Rest and work go together. It is irrelevant to consider them separately because God always places them side by side. They form a dyad that drives a seven-day rhythm: work six, rest one. Twenty-four consecutive hours out of every 168 must be devoted to rest. God even gave that weekly parenthesis a name: the only day of the week not identified simply by a number. He called it the Sabbath.

God's teaching about rest comes in the form of both instruction and example. "Remember the Sabbath day by keeping it holy," He tells us through Moses at the giving of the Ten Commandments. "Six days you shall labor and do all your work, but the seventh day is a Sabbath to the Lord your God. On it you shall not do any work, neither you, nor your son or daughter, nor your manservant or maidservant, nor your animals, nor the alien within your gates. For in six days the Lord made the heavens and the earth, the sea, and all that is in them, but He rested on the seventh day" (Exodus 20:8–11). God apparently knew that simply defining and mandating rest would not be enough to persuade us to practice it. So He modeled it Himself. He created for six days, then rested for one. The implication: if God actually did rest and did not simply command rest, then who are we to ignore the one-day-in-seven time-out?

Three primary words describe the concept of rest in the Old Testament. *Sabat,* the Hebrew word for Sabbath, implies ceasing or coming to the end of an activity. It means to lay down the plow, to put down the pencil, to turn off the computer. *Nuah* adds the dimension of settling down or the absence of movement; it is used to communicate security or a sense of inner ease. It also speaks of a psychological release from pressure and tension, as in the rest from war referred to in Joshua 21:43–44: "So the Lord gave Israel all the land he had sworn to give their forefathers, and they took possession of it and settled there. The Lord gave them rest on every side, just as he had sworn to their forefathers." *Saqat* refers to finding tranquility. It is the kind of rest associated with the absence of external pressure and inner anxiety.

Taken together, the three terms paint rest as a rich and multifaceted concept. Rest involves something we do, something we experience, and something God gives us. We must regularly cease from our work and become still before God. We will gain a sense of tranquility and loose the shackles of stress. God provides supernatural security and peace.

Work *and* Rest, *Not* Work *Versus* Rest

Work is often made to look like a villain in discussions about rest. Work causes things like strain, tension, pressure, and sleepless nights. But rest is the antidote for anything bad caused by work. If work causes sickness, then rest is the cure.

That antagonistic relationship between work and rest is found nowhere in the Bible. God invented both at virtually the same time; they are meant to complement, not fight against, each other. Each contributes something very different to a balanced, integrated life. Without work, life lacks crucial elements that are impossible to gain in any way other than through work. Without rest, we lack what only rest can supply. A biblical connection between rest and work is reflected in word associations such as the following:

REST	WORK
Think	Implement
Reflect	Decide
Slow	Fast
Contentment	Accomplishment
Focus inward	Focus outward
Recharge	Discharge

Sit/Walk	Run/Sprint
Read thoroughly	Scan quickly
Depth	Breadth
Perspective	Productivity

If we don't work:

We are lazy.
We don't provide resources.
We can't fulfill our calling.

If we don't rest:

We are shallow.
We don't assess direction.
We can't worship our God.

A godly life is a life of rest. A godly life is a life of work. Scripture places rest and work side by side and sees them both as good.

Principles *of* Rest

The God who created us to do something (our work calling) also called us to periodically stop that activity (the Sabbath imperative). That model of rest is summarized in the following principles:

1. Rest is an unmistakable priority.

Rest comes up repeatedly in the Old and New Testaments, indicating its importance to God. For example, the prophet Isaiah tells the people of Judah: "If you keep your feet from breaking the Sabbath and from doing as you please on my holy day, if you call the Sabbath a delight and the Lord's holy day honorable, and if you honor it by not going your own way and not doing as you please or speaking idle words, then you will find your joy in the Lord, and I will cause you to ride on the heights of the land and to feast on the inheritance of your father Jacob" (Isaiah 58:13–14).

Likewise, rest was a frequent topic of discussion during Jesus' ministry. He made rest a priority and encouraged his disciples to do the same, even when work demands overwhelmed the amount of time available to accomplish the task. After the disciples returned from their first missions trip, they "gathered around Jesus and reported to Him all they had done and taught. Then, because so many people were coming and going that they didn't even have a chance to eat, He said to them, 'Come with me by yourselves to a quiet place and get some rest'" (Mark 6:30–31).

In *Leisure: Having Fun Is Serious Business* (Multnomah Press, 1981), Charles R. Swindoll points out that "there is not one reference in the entire New Testament saying (or even implying) that Jesus intensely worked and labored in an occupation to the point of emotional exhaustion." Instead, Swindoll notes that "there are several times when we are told He deliberately took a break. . . . His was a life of beautiful balance. He accomplished everything the Father sent Him to do. Everything. And He did it without ignoring those essential times of leisure. If that is the way He lived, then it makes good sense that that is the way we, too, must learn to live."

2.   WORK ALWAYS ATTEMPTS TO INVADE REST.

There is always the pressure and temptation to allow work to spill over into time set aside for rest. That inclination shows up throughout the Scriptures, including in this passage in Nehemiah: "In those days I saw men in Judah treading winepresses on the Sabbath and bringing in grain and loading it on donkeys, together with wine, grapes, figs and all other kinds of loads. And they were bringing all this into Jerusalem on the Sabbath. . . . Men from Tyre who lived in Jerusalem were bringing in fish and all kinds of merchandise and selling them in Jerusalem on the Sabbath to the people of Judah" (Nehemiah 13:15–16).

Nehemiah strongly rebuked the nobles of Judah and took steps to prevent the Sabbath work from continuing. "When evening shadows fell on the gates of Jerusalem before the Sabbath, I ordered the gates of Jerusalem to be shut and not opened until the Sabbath was over. I stationed some of my own men at the gates so that no load could be brought in on the Sabbath day. Once or twice the merchants and sellers of all kinds of goods spent the night outside Jerusalem. But I warned them and said, 'Why do you spend the night by the wall? If you do this again, I will lay hands on you.' From that time on they no longer came on the Sabbath" (Nehemiah 13:19–21).

After the decision is made to rest as scripture describes, there often is a continual struggle to maintain that commitment.

3. Rest requires faith.

It takes faith to not work on the Sabbath—faith to not worry about getting left behind, about getting everything done, or about the pressure to work from peers who don't observe a biblical rest. As with every other part of our life with Christ, rest requires faith. In fact, at the core, the ultimate rest is a faith rest. And a life of faith is always tested in a context where people who don't live by faith seem to do better by violating the tenets of the faith.

We recently met a man who was struggling with this very issue. He faithfully observes and participates in a biblical view of rest, including working only six days a week. His brother has a much different philosophy. He believes that people should run at full speed from the beginning of their careers until they turn forty-five. Only then is there time for devotion to God, family, and leisure. Now in his late thirties, he owns his own company and is making lots of money. He is right on track, at least according to his plan.

The man we talked to thinks his brother is making a huge mistake. He is concerned that his brother's high-stress lifestyle may cause a heart attack before he ever reaches his forty-fifth birthday.

But despite his concerns, our friend wonders if he is missing out. Although he is comfortable with his decision to make rest a priority, he struggles with the fact that he could be making a lot more money if he were more like his brother.

A life with Jesus is a life of faith. And faith inherently means that we trust Jesus with the results of actions that might seem illogical. Rest is no different. Based on the biblical text, rest may take more faith than many other issues we deal with as believers.

Action Plan *for* Rest

What actions should we take to make rest a reality in our life? Following are some simple suggestions drawn from scripture:

1. Break work projects into five- or six-day segments.

Every generation defines the relationship between work and rest differently. Speaking generally, the Builder Generation saw its goal as working with intensity until age sixty-five and then enjoying retirement and rest. The Boomer Generation, though, is perfecting the idea of "early retirement." Put extra hours in closer to the front of a career, and then cash out as soon as possible. Generation Xers see their work less in terms of career and more in terms of projects. Burn the candle at both ends until the project is over, then crash.

In contrast, God's prescription for rest has remained constant since Creation. He requires that we break our work into five- or six-day segments that allow for twenty-four hours of rest. Although few major projects are completed in so few days, arranging the work with real and psychological parentheses of rest allows us to retain biblical balance. The Sabbath rest from work during a project is similar to commas in a sentence. One run-on sentence leaves us breathless, but proper punctuation allows us to read an entire book without running out of energy. A biblical understanding of rest allows us to appropriately budget our schedules and workloads into weeklong portions.

2. CEASE AND DESIST FROM WORK.

Biblical rest means cultivating a lifestyle that includes one day with no work every seventh day. When God first ordained the Sabbath and called it holy, it was not connected with any specific form of worship. Rather, every seventh day was to be set apart from other days by the abstention from all commercial activity. In his book *Love Carved in Stone* (Regal Books, 1983), Daniel R. Seagren explains what this meant: "There would be no tromping on the hot sands, no packing and unpacking of tents, no slaughtering of lambs or cooking, no repair of frazzled goatskins. It would be a day of rest, a change of pace, a day to be eagerly awaited."

The command to lay down the plow is repeated often, from Exodus through Hebrews. All work is to stop for one day every week. God blessed the seventh day because it is special. It is not a consolation prize. The great accomplishments of life are not limited to the first six days of the week. If we never pull away from the assembly line, we will never find rest.

3. REFLECT ON GOD AND CULTIVATE THE INNER PERSON.

In *The Sabbath* (HarperCollins, 1995), Jewish author Abraham Joshua Heschel describes the Sabbath, using lofty and majestic terms: "In the tempestuous ocean of time and toil, there are islands of stillness where man may enter a harbor and reclaim his dignity. The island of the seventh day, the Sabbath, [is] a day of detachment from things, instruments and practical affairs, as well as of attachment to the spirit."

When rest is referenced throughout scripture, it means either to cease from work or to reflect on God, depending on the context. Both reasons for rest have obvious benefits—a break from work and restoration of the soul. In his *Expository Dictionary of Bible Words* (Zondervan, 1985), Larry Richards explains it this way: "Each seventh day provided a full-orbed reminder of who God was to His people. He was the source of their life, He was the provider of their freedom, He was the one who ordered their lives and gave them meaning. The Sabbath day provided a rest from the normal activities of life in the world and an opportunity for each believing Israelite to contemplate his roots and his identity."

4. ALLOW JESUS TO HELP ACCOMPLISH OUR WORK.

Jesus stands, with His arms outstretched, offering to help us with our work. "Come to me, all you who are weary and burdened, and I will give you rest. Take my yoke upon you and learn from me, for I am gentle and humble at heart, and you will find rest for your souls. For my yoke is easy and my burden is light" (Matthew 11:28–30).

That invitation from Jesus gives us permission to make the Sabbath more than merely laying down our work and reflecting on what God has done for us. It allows us to take God's presence in our life one step further—to actually ask for His help in completing our work. Jesus is offering a lifestyle of rest. The picture is one of tranquility, peace, contentment, and fulfillment. The world might be crumbling around us, but when we take Christ's yoke, we experience rest.

Rest is hard work. Good rest is hard to measure. Unlike work, where everything is measured, and measurable, rest is not easily gauged. But if the *act* of rest is difficult to quantify, the *results* of a "Jesus rest" are impossible to ignore.

Such is the story Chuck Colson tells in his classic autobiography *Born Again* (Revell, 1977). During the time near his conversion to Jesus, Colson went to visit his long-time friend Tom Phillips, who was president of the Raytheon Corp. "When I entered his office," Colson writes, "it was the same old Tom, jet-black hair, athletic build, stripped down to shirt-sleeves as always. But the smile was a lot warmer, radiant, in fact, and he looked more relaxed than I had ever seen him. In the old days though always genial, he had had a harried look—with phones ringing, secretaries running in and out of the office, his desk piled high with paper. Now there was something serene about his office as well as about Tom."

The change in Phillips' surroundings and demeanor was dramatic: "There was a new compassion in his eyes and a gentleness in his voice," Colson writes. After about twenty minutes of conversation, Phillips told his friend, "Yes, that's true, Chuck. I have accepted Jesus Christ. I have committed my life to Him and it has been the most marvelous experience of my whole life."

Initially, Colson was shocked by Phillips' response. But the rest and peace the Raytheon executive demonstrated that day played a key role in Colson's conversion several months later.

A lifestyle of biblical rest is just what we need. Demonstration of personal rest in a harried world of work is what everyone wants.

Evaluating Rest

For some reason, the concept of rest rarely makes it into the success stories we read in popular business magazines. Rather, we hear about the people who have sacrificed and have worked around the clock whenever it was needed to build their companies or pursue a dream. The traditional American "pull yourself up by your own bootstraps" approach doesn't take into account any need to pause from hard work. Consider the following questions and take an honest look at your own attitude toward rest. Again, speaking openly with a friend or with members of a small group will help you express your feelings and will challenge you to consider different perspectives.

1. When you hear the term *rest,* what thoughts and emotions come to you?

    Describe your current state now. Are you well rested? Are you worn out and desperately in need of a break? Do you pride yourself on being such a hard worker and on having such high energy that you don't feel the need for rest?

2. WHAT IF SOMEONE CAME TO YOU AND INSISTED THAT YOU TAKE AN EXTENDED VACATION OF AT LEAST TWO WEEKS, PERHAPS EVEN AN ENTIRE MONTH. HOW WOULD YOU REACT—AND WHAT WOULD YOU DO?

Much of our lives tend to be defined by what we do, and the sense that we are "indispensable" somehow gives us a feeling of security. Do you feel useless unless you are actively engaged in some challenging project? Why or why not?

3. HOW ABOUT THE PEOPLE WHO WORK FOR YOU OR WITH YOU? DO YOU MAKE CERTAIN THAT WORK DEMANDS DO NOT INTERFERE WITH THEIR OWN ABILITY TO OBTAIN SUFFICIENT REST?

We may agree with the principle of rest in theory, but it may be difficult to apply in practice, both in our own life and the lives of those with whom we work. A workaholic boss often expects, even demands, the same type of behavior from his or her employees. But is that right?

PRAYING *About* REST

With the hectic, pressure-packed, activity-filled schedules we follow each day, there seems to be little if any place for rest, outside of falling into bed at the end of the day and jumping up as soon as the alarm goes off the next morning. But if God, who created an entire universe and every-thing in it, felt a need for rest, why shouldn't we, since even our most important projects have much less magnitude and importance than His? Let the following prayer guide you toward honestly talking to the Lord about rest and asking Him what He expects you to do.

God, much of the time, it seems that there is no rest for the weary. Even Sundays become jammed with activity, rushing from one church ac-tivity to another, hurrying somewhere for dinner, and then hustling off to something else. Even recreation tends to wear me out. Perhaps I am kid-ding myself, thinking that I am most productive when I am busy, when I might do more in less time if I rested. In Psalm 46:10, You tell us to "be still and know that I am God," and in Psalm 37, You tell us to "be still and wait" on You. Teach me how to do that.

Recommended Resources on Rest

Celebration of Discipline, by Richard J. Foster, HarperCollins, 1978.
Freedom of Simplicity, by Richard J. Foster, HarperCollins, 1981.
Leisure, by Charles R. Swindoll, Multnomah, 1982.
The Sabbath, by Abraham Joshua Heschel, Farrar, Straus & Giroux, 1951.
Sabbath: Restoring the Sacred Rhythm of Rest, by Wayne Muller, Bantam, 1999.
Sabbatical Journey, by Henri J. M. Nouwen, Crossroads, 1998.
Time Off Work: Using Sabbaticals to Enhance Your Life While Keeping Your Career on Track, by Lisa Angowski, Wiley, 1994.
When I Relax I Feel Guilty, by Tim Hansel, Cook, 1984.

More Than a Dreamer

Sherri sat in her office late one evening. Everyone else had left hours before, but she sat quietly at her computer, glancing through e-mail, visiting a couple of Web sites that plotted current business trends, and jotting random notes on a pad in front of her. Her executive placement firm had grown tremendously over the past four years, but Sherri was never one to stand pat—in business or in a friendly game of cards. What will it take to improve on what we have?

As a "head hunter," she had experienced her share of both feast and famine, first on the staff of a major national recruiting firm and then as the head of her own company. Things were going okay now, but what about tomorrow, next week, . . . or next year? Sherri remembered a comment she had heard years before from a noted leader: "You're either getting better or you're getting worse." Accepting both better and worse might work in marriage, but she didn't think it had a place in business— at least not one that one wanted to keep going.

Even though her business had been recognized as one of the rising stars in the region, she wondered what she could do to strengthen her firm for future uncertainties. Were there any strategic measures that she should be considering? What about her own effectiveness? Should she be doing something to make herself a more effective leader for her team? Sherri had often heard about strategic planning, but was there such a thing as strategic *doing*?

Not having a crystal ball—and not believing in them anyway—she had no way of knowing for certain what the future held, such as what business trends would have a significant impact on her company, what new technology she should prepare for, or even who her new competitors might be. "Only God knows," she thought to herself, quickly realizing the truth of that idea. Then she recalled a Bible verse she had learned years before—almost as if someone had just reached into a file folder and pulled it out. It was from Proverbs and said, "Commit to the Lord whatever you do, and your plans will succeed."

"Well, I'm not sure what it is that I should be doing, but committing it to the Lord sounds like a strategic first step!" she decided.

■ ■

Joseph, one of the Old Testament patriarchs, was born to lead. According to Genesis, he was "well-built and handsome." He was also athletic and intelligent. And his supernatural ability to interpret dreams, combined with his boldness, enabled him to tell their meaning, regardless of how that stunning truth would affect his listeners. It's no wonder he was the favorite of his father's many sons.

Amazingly, Joseph was not a proud man. He did not allow his obvious talents to go to his head. Neither did he become bitter, even though he endured tremendous injustices—at the hands of his brothers and also because of the slanderous accusation brought against him by the wife of Egyptian officer Potiphar. Despite his undeserved years in jail, Joseph did not compromise his character or his trust in God. He is one of the few men in the Bible about whom nothing negative is recorded.

Dealing with every stumbling block that was thrown into his path, Joseph rose in only thirteen years from being a shepherd to holding the second most powerful position on the planet—serving as second in command to the Pharaoh of Egypt—a ruler and a nation that dominated the world in that day. As a result, God used Joseph to implement a fourteen-year strategic plan that saved millions of people from a deadly famine. Joseph was a *strategic leader,* from whom we can learn much.

The terms *strategy* and *leader* are virtually inseparable. Our word *strategy* comes from a group of Greek terms that refer to military and civilian leadership, as well as to combat operations. For example, in

Acts 4:1, the captain of the temple guard is identified as the *strategos* in the Greek text. That same word is used again in Revelation 19:19 to identify Jesus, when He arrives in triumph on a white horse to rescue His followers and throw Satan into hell. According to both ancient Greek literature and the Scriptures, one must be strategic in order to be a genuine leader. Leadership unconnected to strategy was not considered to be leadership at all.

But strategy is a rich word that refers to more than just leadership. In its full scope, strategy also refers to moving an enterprise forward in a planned and coordinated way. When Proverbs 30:27 states that "locusts have no king, yet they advance together in ranks," the picture is of unified progress. Strategy advances an organization at the correct pace toward a meaningful vision with an integrated plan.

Thus, genuine leadership is always strategic, and strategic leadership always means taking an enterprise toward a better future, using a cohesive blueprint. With that as background, it is no mystery why the concept of strategy has been widely adapted from government and military contexts to the world of business.

As we study the biblical account of Joseph's life, we see that eight qualities emerged from his life and career as a strategic leader:

1.   A STRATEGIC LEADER NURTURES INNER HEALTH DESPITE
      EXTERNAL ORDEALS.

Joseph had a tough early career. Perhaps because his father, Jacob, seemed to show him preferential treatment, his brothers hated him; spurred by their jealousy, they conspired to murder him. Their long-awaited opportunity came one day when Joseph was sent by his father to check on the well-being of the brothers while they were tending the family's sheep. According to Genesis 37:19–20, the brothers saw Joseph approaching in the distance and schemed to kill him, throw him into an empty cistern, and then lie to their father, telling him that a wild animal had devoured Joseph. But instead of killing Joseph, the brothers were prompted to revise their plan and decided instead to sell him as a slave to a group of merchants who would take him to Egypt.

In Egypt, Joseph was sold to Potiphar, one of Pharaoh's top officials. Before long, Joseph showed himself to be a hardworking, responsible, and trustworthy individual (Genesis 39:3–6). This caught the eye of the Egyptian officer, who made Joseph his chief attendant, placing him in charge of everything he owned. God's hand of blessing was on Joseph, and Potiphar's confidence was rewarded as he saw everything prosper under his trusted servant's care. Unfortunately, Joseph also caught the eye of Potiphar's wife, who decided she wanted to become much more closely acquainted with him. However, when he spurned her immoral advances, she falsely accused him of rape. Despite Joseph's flawless track record of integrity and commitment, Potiphar chose to believe his wife's allegations. As a result, Joseph was thrown into prison, guilty of nothing except being a loyal servant to his master, and there he remained virtually forgotten for years.

Imagine how life must have seemed for Joseph at that point. He was a young man rejected by his brothers, sold into slavery, trapped in a foreign country, and imprisoned for a crime he never committed. His personal experience was terrible. But his private life was clean.

Scripture is clear that Joseph steadfastly refused to become violent, irate, resentful, or vindictive. Instead of succumbing to his circumstances, he succeeded in soaring above them. He was an effective leader precisely because he was free of inner turmoil. What could have become a personal maelstrom for Joseph instead remained a life controlled by tranquility and peace.

Strength of leadership is diminished when bitterness and hostility take up private residence in a leader's life. Decisions that emanate from this deadly mix have the potential of carrying out anger and vengeance, even if the leader outwardly seems calm and calculated. They often prove to be bad decisions, although their detrimental results may not be obvious until much later.

Jesus had strong words for leaders who pretend to have it together but in reality are full of inner garbage: "Woe to you, teachers of the Law and Pharisees, you hypocrites! You are like whitewashed tombs, which look beautiful on the outside but on the inside are full of dead men's bones and everything unclean. In the same way, on the outside you appear to people as righteous but on the inside you are full of hypocrisy and wickedness" (Matthew 23:27–28).

So much of sustained leadership is built on the principle of leaders being at peace with themselves. If there is a civil war raging in the chest and mind of a leader, it will have consequences. Cultivating and caring for the inner person is crucial. Having a strong moral center, maintaining a clear mental path, cultivating a healthy emotional framework, and sustaining a vital internal spirit: these are all essential to being a strategic leader.

2. A STRATEGIC LEADER SOLVES PROBLEMS WITHOUT ENGAGING IN SELF-PROMOTION.

One night, while Joseph languished in jail, Pharaoh had a dream. The ruler's mystic consultants were summoned to decipher the message, but none of them was able to explain the vision. Based on a recommendation from his chief cupbearer, who remembered having a dream of his own perfectly interpreted years ago while he was in prison, Pharaoh sent for Joseph, hoping he could determine the dream's meaning.

Joseph stunned Pharaoh after hearing the Egyptian king relate the details of his vision. Not only was he able to tell what the dream meant, stating that God had enabled him to understand that it concerned a forthcoming catastrophic crop failure, but he could also outline a strategy that would help the leader of Egypt prepare for his country's coming famine. Joseph, however, did not try to convince Pharaoh to hire him to implement the plan: "And now let Pharaoh look for a discerning and wise man and put him in charge of the land of Egypt. Let Pharaoh appoint commissioners over the land to take a fifth of the harvest of Egypt during the seven years of abundance. They should collect all the food of these good years that are coming and store up the grain under the authority of Pharaoh, to be kept in the cities for food. This food should be held in reserve for the country, to be used during the seven years of famine that will come upon Egypt, so that the country may not be ruined by the famine" (Genesis 41:33–36).

Self-promoters seem to be everywhere and are easy to identify, but they do not command respect. Even after Joseph was hired by Pharaoh and successfully oversaw one of the largest human aid projects in history, he consistently gave God the glory for his accomplishments, taking none of the credit for himself. This attitude is evident in Genesis 50:20, when he told his brothers, "You intended to harm me, but God intended it for good to accomplish what is now being done, the saving of many lives."

Maintaining a humble perspective like this is especially difficult for a salesman who is promotional by nature, seeking to convince that what he has to offer is by far the best. It's also difficult for people who are hungry for business. But strategic leaders seem to lead with both hands and both eyes, with both the organization and the task in front of them. Leaders cease to be strategic when they fix their eyes on their own egos and aspirations.

3. A STRATEGIC LEADER IDENTIFIES UPCOMING BENDS IN THE BUSINESS.

Joseph was gifted in looking toward the future and anticipating unforeseen twists and turns. Inevitable curves such as these can come from within the organization as well as from outside. But regardless of their origin, they have a significant effect on any enterprise.

The following scenario could be applied to hundreds of businesses across the country. A family company needs to orchestrate a transition from one generation of leadership to the next. It proves successful, resulting in annual sales of about $500 million, the company's highest ever. But the owners are having trouble keeping up with the changes going on around them; their leadership team is tired and somewhat out of date. Part of the problem is that their industry is going through tremendous consolidation, dramatically affecting the rules of the game and altering the nature of their competition. In addition, overproduction has knocked the supply and demand curve out of kilter.

If Joseph were around to help, he would be able to gaze into the company's future and help the owners create a path along which he could envision where coming events would take them. This is what he did for Pharaoh. Through the Egyptian leader's dream, Joseph saw what the professional seers were unable to comprehend; he realized that the next fourteen years would present tremendous challenges for Egypt and the world as food supplies soared to all-time highs and then faded to nothing at all.

This ability to identify upcoming bends in the business is a gift. Either someone has it or he doesn't. Reading the tea leaves after the fact isn't that difficult, but having the intuitive sense to look down the road and feel around the corner is an unusual ability that cannot be learned, nor can it be acquired through hard work or wishful thinking. Those who don't have this gift are not disqualified from leadership, but they need to surround themselves with people—consultants, employees, or board members—who have this innate ability to anticipate inevitable twists and turns and then discern what appropriate steps must be taken to handle them properly and successfully.

Peter Drucker suggests, in *Managing in Turbulent Times* (Harper-Business, 1993), that anticipation is one of the most important managerial skills one can possess during times of turbulence. Many successful managers and leaders have strong problem-solving skills, which they employ primarily in a reactive mode. However, approaching business issues proactively—before a crisis sets in—makes the twists and turns easier to handle.

4. A STRATEGIC LEADER ANALYZES AND CONNECTS INFORMATION.

To sort, size, critique, categorize, connect, and link information means realizing that not everything goes into the same bucket. This isn't always easy; in fact, sometimes we have to make hairline distinctions. To "size" means to consider the expected impact, as well as the unintended consequences, of our proposed actions. And to connect, of course, means to figure out how various pieces of the puzzle fit together. In other words, we must use a systematic approach to come up with a workable solution.

Pharaoh's dream revealed that Egypt was about to experience seven years of great abundance, followed by seven years of severe famine (Genesis 41:29–31). Joseph could have stopped with the raw interpretation, but he went further than that. By analyzing and connecting the information he gave to Pharaoh, Joseph drew conclusions that made his interpretation much more valuable and practical. When he was finished talking, Pharaoh knew what action was needed to avoid disaster over the next fourteen years. Instead of becoming only a part of the looming problem, he became part of its solution.

5. A STRATEGIC LEADER MAKES WISE DECISIONS.

Joseph's brothers were not good decision makers. In fact, problems seemed to paralyze their thinking. They might still be standing there looking at each other if their father had not pushed them to go to Egypt for food. "When Jacob learned that there was grain in Egypt, he said to his sons, 'Why do you just keep looking at each other? I have heard that there is grain in Egypt. Go down there and buy some for us, so that we may live and not die'" (Genesis 42:1–2).

Wisdom in making decisions lies somewhere between being impulsive and being hesitant. Every leader must be willing to make decisions, regardless of how hard they are to reach and implement. The "ready, aim, aim, aim" syndrome will not work. Leaders must be willing to fire.

Andrew Carnegie stated it this way: "It has been my experience that a man who cannot reach a decision promptly once he has all the necessary facts for the decision at hand cannot be depended upon to carry through any decision he may make. I have also discovered that men who reach decisions promptly usually have the capacity to move with definiteness of purpose in other circumstances."

6.   A STRATEGIC LEADER USES PERSONAL GIFTS TO DEFINE
      LEADERSHIP STYLE.

Joseph was a gifted manager, and that personal passion was evident whether he was dealing with people or projects. Potiphar recognized this gift almost immediately. As a result, he installed the young man over his entire household and everything he owned (Genesis 39:4). Later, the prison warden perceived that special managerial ability, and Joseph was entrusted with the responsibility for all of the other prisoners (Genesis 39:22). Finally, Pharaoh's confirmation of Joseph's unique skill landed the thirty-year-old former shepherd an appointment to serve as chief executive of Egypt (Genesis 41:41).

Many leaders go through life trying to become something they're not, which is unfortunate, because there is no prototype of what a great leader ought to look like. Recognizing and capitalizing on personal gifts, whatever they may be, is the key to being effective. It helps answer such questions as how the leader fits into an organization, what kind of a team needs to be assembled, and how to most effectively allocate time for both people and projects.

7.   A STRATEGIC LEADER FOLLOWS THROUGH TO IMPLEMENTATION.

Strategic leaders have the ability to provide focus, and once the plans are in place, they follow through until the work is completed. Joseph, for example, placed great emphasis on following through. After he had formulated the plan for feeding the people of Egypt during the years of famine, he launched into clear, decisive action: "Joseph collected all the food produced in those seven years of abundance in Egypt and stored it in the cities. . . . Joseph stored up huge quantities of grain, like the sand of the sea; it was so much that he stopped keeping records because it was beyond measure" (Genesis 41: 48–49).

Effective leaders do more that just come up with ideas. Effective leaders also prove that they are able to deliver the goods. One wise business sage said it this way: "All good ideas are eventually reduced to a pile of hard work for someone." In Joseph's case, this meant assembling and mobilizing a team of workers who would first collect the surplus grain during the years of plenty and then begin distributing them back to the people during the following years of want.

8. A STRATEGIC LEADER REINVENTS THE VISION.

Several years into the famine, Joseph still had plenty of grain left. But the people of Egypt and Canaan were out of money. So Joseph adjusted his business plan and gave them grain in exchange for their livestock. Next, he traded them grain for land. Being the wise leader that he was, Joseph adapted to the changing market environment and was able to continue his plan with nary a hiccup.

The same holds true for the business world of the twenty-first century. Strategic leaders must revise their plans as new challenges arise and new opportunities present themselves. In reality, however, while some companies reinvent their vision and change with the times, others do not, or, due to poor leadership, cannot. According to an article in *Forbes* (June, 1997), only fifteen of the largest hundred American companies in 1917 remained in business eight decades later. AT&T, Citicorp, DuPont, General Electric, Kodak, Procter & Gamble, and Sears had survived, along with six oil companies and two automakers. The other eighty-five, however, went bankrupt, were purchased, merged with other companies, or just closed their doors. When the picture of reality changes, so does the vision for the future.

STRATEGY IS DEEPLY ROOTED, *Not a* PASSING FAD

Strategy is more than a great business word. It is not a trend or a fad or a passing whim. Strategy is a concept rooted deeply in the Scriptures, both in definition and in illustration.

Regarding definition, strategy refers to a thinking leader who is able to advance an enterprise in a planned and coordinated way. Strategic leaders embody such words as vision, integration, implementation, anticipation, clarity, flexibility, skill, and passion.

Regarding illustration, the example Joseph set supplies volumes of material for drawing a detailed picture of strategic leadership. Joseph was to strategic leadership what a paint-by-number project is to kids. His example guides us through the biblical definition of leadership by living out principles that we understand because we can see. Joseph is a case study of strategic leadership, one from which we can glean as many practical principles for today's world of commerce as we could find in any M.B.A. class offered at an Ivy League college.

Evaluating Strategy

Many leaders like to work according to a clearly articulated plan. Others prefer a plan that leaves room for ambiguity—knowing that sudden, unexpected changes or shifts in the environment around them can turn even the most thoughtfully constructed plan upside down. But not all leaders are truly strategic, looking far enough down the road to prepare for future needs and developments while not neglecting present realities. How strategic are you? This may not be a question you have seriously asked yourself, but, based on what you have found in this chapter, prepare to share with someone your thoughts on this topic of strategy:

1. Explain your understanding of "strategic leadership" as it is discussed in this chapter. Do you agree with this view?

    Can you think of someone you know who would qualify as a strategic leader? How well do the eight qualities of a strategic leader apply to you personally?

2. What are some of the factors that can hinder true strategic leadership in today's business environment?

    How could the "tyranny of the urgent" we all face, seemingly every day, deter leaders from taking a strategic approach in their roles? What would it take to promote a much stronger emphasis on strategic decision making—and strategic action?

3. Do you think being a follower of Jesus Christ places a higher premium on strategic leadership? Why or why not?

    In considering the life of Christ, give some examples of ways in which He led strategically. Think of one area that, if you approached it more strategically, could greatly increase your impact as a representative of Christ in the workplace.

Praying *About* Strategy

Often, instead of making life "happen," it just seems to happen to us. We react to life rather than taking a more strategic, proactive approach, whether it is at work, in the home, or in our community. Yet in the Scriptures, as we examine the lives of leaders God used most fruitfully, we see that much of what they did was truly strategic, with an eye toward the future, ultimately to eternity. Would you like to be a strategic vessel for God's purposes? Then consider the following prayer to talk about this with Him.

God, as I review the sum total of each day, it seems that so much of what I do is anything but strategic. I'm handling "emergencies" and putting out fires, but I'm rarely thinking or acting in ways that will make a positive, profound difference. Give me a sense of how I can think and act to have a greater impact for You where I work, in my home, in my neighborhood, and in the city. Enable me to be more like Joseph—or Nehemiah—someone whose strategy carries out a meaningful vision and an integrated plan, ultimately for Your glory.

Recommended Resources on Strategy

Built to Last, by James C. Collins and Jerry I. Porras, Harper Business, 1994.
Good to Great, by James C. Collins, Harper Business, 2001.
Strategy Pure and Simple: How Winning CEOs Outthink Their Competition, by Michel Robert, McGraw-Hill, 1993.

C H A P T E R

Taking a New Look
at Innovation

Being around Chelsea was a continuing adventure in the unexpected. Whether she was at home, on an outing with friends, or at work, she always seemed engaged in a search for something fresh and new. So when her oldest friend, Tina, stepped into her office, she was shocked to see the usually bubbly, upbeat Chelsea sitting at her desk, face tied into a frown as she randomly shuffled some papers.

"What's wrong, Chels?" Tina asked. "Computer network down? Your voice mail develop laryngitis?"

"No," Chelsea answered with a sigh. "I'm just frustrated. Over the last three days I have presented five ideas that I think could greatly increase our department's productivity, and every time, Watkins has poured ice water on them. If he says one more time, 'If it ain't broken, don't fix it,' I think I'll show him something that's broken! I'm not trying to run the department, but if there are ways of doing things better and more efficiently, what's wrong with that?"

"Nothing that I know of," Tina replied. "But you know—people are afraid of something new, especially when they didn't think of it themselves. I remember the first time someone asked me about using a computer. I had been perfectly content with my electric typewriter and couldn't imagine why I would want to go to the trouble of converting to word processing. But you know what? Within two days, I was convinced.

Suddenly, my old faithful typewriter seemed about as efficient as carving in stone. I wouldn't give up my computer now and switch back to a typewriter if you offered me a million dollars. Well, $500,000, anyway."

"Yes, I know. Innovation can be scary. But where would we be without it? I'm just trying to help. Forgive me for saying this, but I think some of my ideas can really make a difference. But it's not a matter of getting the credit. All I want to know is, how can I get others to see that?"

"I know your ideas are good," Tina agreed. "You're a walking, talking idea machine. But sometimes you're so zealous about them, you come on as strong as a field of garlic. Why don't you down-key it a bit, give people time to absorb what you're proposing, and maybe even present them in such a way that they will decide that it was their idea in the first place? If you're not concerned about who gets the credit, what does it matter, right?"

■ ■

Innovation is the cornerstone of modern civilization. It is so intertwined in our daily lives—by way of a steady stream of new ideas, products, technologies, and services—that we virtually take it for granted. Consider the advancements that have been made in the area of word processing, for example. We've gone from manual to electric typewriters and from manual to voice-recognition computers—all within a single lifetime. And that's just one of innumerable quantum leaps of progress that have taken place in recent years.

The word *innovate* comes from a fifteenth-century Middle-French word meaning renewal or a new way of doing things. Like a snowball rolling down a hill that gathers both momentum and mass as it continues, innovation reached such a prominent place in society at large—and in the business community, specifically—that historians describe the nineteenth century as the age of "the invention of inventions." In the twentieth century, the conviction that innovation was the key to progress became so ingrained in our thinking that we took the work that used to be done by eccentric inventors in basement laboratories and we institutionalized it through corporate research and development departments.

Sixty-nine of 301 companies profiled in *The Mission Statement Book* by Jeffrey Abrahams (Ten Speed Press, 1995) refer to innovation in their mission statements. Most of those companies also list innovation as one of their core values. Regardless of whether the word and concept are part of a formal mission statement, companies today believe in innovation and consider it crucial for organizational success. Even if the word doesn't show up in a corporate mission statement, innovation certainly holds high value in our culture. Business periodicals are full of articles about improvements and innovations—from supply chain management technology that allows for continuous replenishment of shelves in retail stores to new methods of recruiting and retaining employees.

Our current environment of innovation has not always existed. The ancient Greeks were masters at speculating about the past through their poetry and their philosophy, but they seldom thought about the future. In his landmark book *The Creators* (Random House, 1992), Daniel J. Boorstin writes that "the typical Greek thinker has been called a 'backward-looking animal.'" With their cyclical view of history, the Greeks were essentially pessimists who believed that the advancement of civilization brought new problems and complications.

That was the historical framework for the life of Jesus Christ. And even with the advent of the good news of the gospel, including the amazing proclamation that men and women were not prisoners of their past but could be redeemed, and that history was not doomed to repeat itself in cycles but instead was heading toward an end point of the Second Coming of Christ, the culture at large remained mired in the view that significant progress was not realistically possible.

Early Christian writers attacked the idea that material progress was impossible, but it was not until Augustine published his influential book *The City of God,* in 426 A.D., that society's view began to shift toward a more Christ-centered and optimistic view of progress and innovation. According to Augustine, "history was revealed not as an 'eternal return' but as an eternal movement, to fulfill the promise announced by the coming of Christ." It was in that context that Augustine hammered the point of a God-infused creativity in men and women:

> Man's invention has brought forth so many in such rare sciences and arts that the excellency of his capacity makes a rare goodness of his creation apparent . . . and shows from what an

excellent gift he has those inventions and practices of his. . . . What varieties has man found out in buildings, attires, husbandry, navigation, sculpture, and painting! What perfection he has shown in the shows of theatres, in painting, killing and catching wild beasts! . . . . What thousands of medicines for the health, of meat for the pallet, of means and figures to persuade, of eloquent phrases to delight, of verses for pleasure, of musical inventions and instruments! . . . How large is the capacity of man, if we should dwell upon particulars! (*The City of God,* 426 A.D.).

Boorstin contends that *The City of God* provided the foundation that led to our modern idea of progress. But from where did Augustine draw his theology of progress and innovation?

The first verb in the first chapter of the first book in the Bible is *bana,* the Hebrew word for "create." "In the beginning God created . . ." (Genesis 1:1). Before we leave the first two chapters of Genesis, God awes us with His singular and spectacular ability to create from nothing—to begin with a blank canvas and speak into existence everything in the heavens and on the earth. At the outset, we're introduced to this attribute of God that is both highly visible and of primary importance throughout the Bible. The same word in Greek is used throughout scripture to describe God's work in initiating the plan of salvation, in initiating new heavens, a new earth, and a new Jerusalem at the end of time, and in initiating peace.

A key aspect of understanding how a creative God connects with the creativity and innovation of the men and women He created can be found in Genesis 1:27: "So God created man in His own image, in the image of God He created him, male and female He created them." The logic is clear. A God with creativity as a primary attribute created men and women in His image. In other words, our creativity comes from God because He has endowed us with a measure of who He is. We were created in God's image. Intrinsic within every man and woman, therefore, is a measure of creativity and innovation. It shows itself in different ways, but it is always present. God created us to be innovative.

It was precisely the innovation displayed by Jesus, the infinite God-man, which caused so much controversy among the people of His day. Key to our understanding of Jesus' teaching on innovation is a statement he made early in His public ministry: "No one sows a patch of unshrunk cloth on an old garment, for the patch will pull away from the garment, making the tear worse. Neither do men pour new wine into old wineskins. If they do, the skins will burst, the wine will run out and the wineskins will be ruined. No, they pour new wine into new wineskins, and both are preserved" (Matthew 9:16–17).

Following his usual teaching style, Jesus pulls two illustrations from daily life to make a point to His newly formed leadership team. The first illustration involved sewing a new piece of wool to a coat that had seen better days; the second illustration involved placing new wine in an old container. William Hendriksen paints the full picture of the wine and the wineskins:

> The wine skin was usually made of the skin of a goat or sheep. After being removed from the animal, it was tanned, and after the hair had been cut close the skin was turned inside out. The neck opening became the mouth of "the bottle." The other openings, at the feet and the tail, were closed with cords. Naturally an old wineskin is no match for the new, still-fermenting wine, for such wine tends to stretch the container. A new wineskin would be sufficiently elastic to stand the pressure, but under similar conditions an old one, stiff and rigid, would crack. The wine would spill out and the skin would be of no further use (*New Testament Commentary: Exposition of the Gospel According to Matthew,* Baker Book House, 1982).

In this passage, the case is made that there are times when innovation—something new—is necessary. William Barclay, in his commentary *The Gospel of Matthew* (Westminster, 1975), points out that "no one would willingly or recklessly . . . abandon what has stood the test of time . . . but the fact remains that this is a growing and expanding universe; and there comes a time when patches are useless." He goes on to suggest that "our minds must be elastic enough to receive and contain new ideas." Every new idea has had to battle for existence against the instinctive opposition of the human mind. In the beginning, the automobile, the railway train, and the airplane were all regarded with suspicion. Even Jonas Hanaway, who brought the umbrella to the United States, had to suffer a barrage of insults the first time he walked down the street with it.

Two principles of innovation can be found in Matthew 9:16–17. First, *the possibility for something new always exists.* At His core, Jesus is all about making old things new; after all, He came to establish a New Covenant. New is assumed in this passage. It is assumed that there will be new cloth, and it is assumed that there will be new wine.

Second, *innovation is about initiating something new,* and that is precisely what Jesus did. Early in His ministry, during His first opportunity to teach His newly chosen disciples what the good news he was proclaiming meant, Jesus launched into the Sermon on the Mount (Matthew 5–7). This was his first opportunity to teach his new team, and the refrain during that initial training seminar was, "You have heard that it was said. . . . But I tell you that." Jesus repeated that chorus six times as he expanded on earlier teachings about murder, adultery, divorce, oaths, revenge, and love for enemies. In every case, He explained with firm precision what this New Covenant included.

This is a distinctively Christ-like message. The words *God, optimism,* and *hope* belong together. Inherent in the mind-set of a follower of Christ is the understanding that the new really can happen. Just ask Nicodemus, who learned firsthand that redemption requires rebirth (John 3:1–8). If we don't believe that new things can happen, we don't believe redemption is possible. But we have been born again; we have been renewed.

Based on that truth, the following three rules govern the game of how we must approach innovation:

1. REALISM IS IN; CYNICISM IS OUT.
    A cynical mindset is one that sits back and torpedoes new ideas. Cynics really don't believe that anything will change or that anything good or new will really happen. Followers of Christ have little room for cynicism; they do, however, have an obligation to view an innovative proposal realistically. Can it really happen? Does the opportunity really exist? Is the mechanism in place that will allow it to flourish?

2. REASON IS IN; THE UNWILLINGNESS TO BE PERSUADED IS OUT.
    I have every right and obligation to marshal all available powers of reason to my aid in evaluating an innovative or creative proposal. I do not, however, have the option of intransigence unless I am dealing in an area of ethical or moral wrongdoing. My job is to reason with a

mind open enough to accept the possibility of innovation if it proves to be a reasonable alternative to the status quo.

3.   HISTORY IS IN; HISTORY ALONE IS OUT.

Precedent can be a wonderful evaluator of future success, but it is not the only piece of equipment in our arsenal of assessment tools. If history were the only thing we used to predict the future, then we would be guilty of the same cycle that trapped the ancient Greeks. History is not unimportant, but it's not all-important either.

INNOVATION IS SYSTEMIC

Jesus' illustration makes it clear that a piece of new fabric won't repair an old coat very well, and that old wineskins won't hold new wine. In other words, in order for a new patch to be successful, it must be connected to a new coat. By the same token, new wine belongs in new wineskins. Any discussion of innovation must include an understanding of how the new thing—whatever it is—fits in its proposed context. Innovation needs to be protected and incubated. It does not happen in a vacuum. In elementary school, children are given tests that ask them to match various objects—a picture of a winter scarf with the image of a snowman, for example. The same matching principle applies to innovation. To ensure its success, an innovation must be surrounded by the proper elements.

In *Innovation and Entrepreneurship* (Harper & Row, 1985), Peter Drucker points out that Leonardo da Vinci was one of the most brilliant inventive geniuses the world has ever known. Although he lived in the 1500s—long before the age of modern machinery, his notebooks were full of drawings about futuristic things, such as helicopters and submarines. But it would be three hundred to four hundred years before any of those great ideas actually hit the skies or the seas. That's because a good idea by itself is not enough. A great idea at the wrong time is not a bad thing, but it probably won't result in innovation.

Over the last few decades, business technology has trained us to think systemically—to understand process and to be aware of how one thing in a system affects another. That mind-set won't cause innovation by itself, but it is necessary if innovation is to happen. With that in mind, consider the following questions when you're contemplating an idea that could grow into a successful innovation:

- What technology will be required to launch and sustain the innovation?

Does that technology already exist? Is it readily available? Is there some kind of preliminary technological work that must be accomplished in order to connect the dots between this idea and the marketplace?

- What resources will be required to begin and continue the innovation?

We have only so much time, so much money, and so many people. Do we have enough of each of these, not only to get the new idea off the ground but also to keep it going over time?

- What structure will be required to launch and sustain the innovation?

The organizational structure, or the environment within which an innovation thrives, is often far different from a structure that has allowed prior ideas to work. Sometimes, a complete divorce from the current situation is necessary before an innovation can flourish. At other times, a parallel organization that differs from the original organization in just a few ways can be an adequate environment for the innovation. What we need to consider is whether the innovation under consideration would work in the original environment.

- When will the time be right?

Is this the right time for this idea to happen? What specific characteristics lead to the conclusion that now is or is not an appropriate time?

- Who will provide appropriate leadership?

Nothing happens without a leader. Someone must champion the innovation and continue to lead it after it's launched.

The old wineskin and the old coat are but two items Jesus used to demonstrate innovation during His earthly ministry. From turning water into wine (John 2:1–10) and using mud to heal a blind man's eyes (John 9:1–7) to feeding huge crowds of people with a child's lunch (Mark 6:35–44) and teaching His disciples a lesson on faith by walking on water (Matthew 14:22–32), Jesus always found creative ways get His message across.

Many people who lived in Jesus' day were drawn to Him because they wanted to see Him perform miracles and hear Him teach. And on their quest to see the Master Innovator in action, some of these people had to be quite innovative themselves. Take Zacchaeus, for example. He certainly wasn't the only short guy in Jericho, but according to Luke 19:1–6, he was the only one creative enough to climb a tree so that he could catch a glimpse of Christ.

Then there were the four men who were trying to help their friend, the paralytic, get to Jesus so that he could be healed. Mark 2:3–5 describes how they cut a hole in the roof of the building where Jesus was teaching and lowered the paralyzed man down through the opening. Talk about an innovative way to beat the crowds!

Moving out of the Gospels, we come upon an example of innovation that shows what the answers to the questions about technology, resources, structure, timing, and leadership could look like when applied to a specific situation—in this case, the creation and organization of the early church.

The answer to the timing question is obvious. For three years, the disciples and other believers had been under the day-to-day leadership of Jesus. But they needed a new structure under which to operate after He ascended into heaven. The technology question doesn't really apply to this scenario, but the issue of resources certainly does. The approach that the believers took—pooling and sharing all their possessions—allowed them to maintain their "one-heart, one mind" spirit (Acts 4:32–35). It was also an innovative way to make sure that everyone's needs were met.

As far as structure was concerned, the group had no choice but to come up with a new way of doing things, because their leader, Jesus, was no longer with them in person. Led by the Holy Spirit, the apostles were in charge of setting up the ministry of the church. But when it became clear that they needed assistance with such tasks as oversee-ing food distribution (Acts 6:1–6), they revamped their organizational structure to include seven leaders who would be responsible for meet-ing physical needs. By doing so, they helped ensure that the church would continue to grow and flourish.

Finally, when it came to leadership, the early church was blessed with leaders who had been trained by the one true servant leader, Jesus Christ. When the church was established, Peter played a leading role, along with the other apostles and believers who had followed Jesus throughout his ministry. Paul came on the scene later and started planting churches throughout the world. The very fact that the church was able to expand and grow suggests that these leaders were not afraid to try new things, from taking the gospel to the Gentiles to commu-nicating the message of grace to the Jewish people.

Their methods were innovative, but, more important, their mes-sage was revolutionary. The men and women of the early church, who had been created in the image of a creative God, were living examples of the new creation, as stated in 2 Corinthians 5:17: "Therefore, if anyone is in Christ, he is a new creation; the old has gone, the new has come!"

A Special Word *About* Innovation

Creative ideas provide the spark that lights the fire of innovation, but the flames die unless the ideas are nurtured under the right circum-stances. This chapter has identified five essential components for keep-ing that fire of innovation burning. *Diffusion of Innovations,* by Everett M. Rogers (Free Press, 1995), is filled with real examples of how this has played out for various businesses. Here are some of them:

Technology

The facsimile machine was invented in 1843 by Alexander Bain, a Scottish clock maker. But it took another 150 years—when the ap-propriate telephone infrastructure was in place—for the fax machine to became an essential piece of office equipment.

The first fax machine transmitted messages over telegraph lines. In 1948, RCA introduced a version that used radio waves. Two decades later, Xerox made a fax machine called a telecopier, which used telephone lines to send photographs and articles to newspapers. But accessing phone lines still required operator assistance, so the use of fax machines remained limited.

Automatic dialing and direct connection of fax machines to regular phone lines came next, but it wasn't until the early 1980s—when transmission speed had increased and the price had dropped—that companies in the United States began to use fax machines. Today, the concept that Bain developed costs only a few hundred dollars and can be found in just about every office in the country.

Resources

American Airlines developed the computerized reservation system in a way that exemplifies how a company must develop resources before implementing an innovation. In conjunction with IBM, American Airlines developed a reservation system that matched passengers to seats, printed travel itineraries, issued boarding passes, and moved reservations terminals to travel agencies. It took another twenty years for airline employees to amass the technical expertise needed to run the new system, named SABRE.

The results far exceeded American Airlines' expectations. "The first 200 installations had been expected to contribute $3.1 million in increased passenger sales per year; the actual contribution was $20 million, a return on investment of 500 percent," Rogers writes in *Diffusion of Innovations*.

Structure

When Thermos Corporation created its Thermal Electric Grill, a product that allowed the company to increase its share of the electric grill market from 2 to 20 percent the first year it was sold, the product's success was due in part to a dramatic change in corporate structure.

In 1990, the CEO of Thermos decided to replace the company's traditional bureaucratic organizational structure—divisions for engineering, manufacturing, marketing, and so forth—with flexible, interdisciplinary work teams. The Thermal Electric Grill was the first product Thermos designed under this new system, and the project was so successful that the company has since adopted the concept of flexible work groups to create other new products.

Timing

Timing played a key role in the introduction of the Nintendo home video game-player to the U.S. market. Nintendo's predecessor, the Atari game-player, was introduced in 1972. But, according to Rogers, poor management led to excessively rapid growth, and poor product quality left a bad taste with consumers.

By producing an advanced game-player that would only accept game cartridges made by Nintendo, the company was able to monopolize the industry in Japan. Nintendo officials knew that it would be tough to introduce a new video game-player in the United States, but in 1986, only two years after Atari went bankrupt, they launched the product in New York. Their gamble on the timing, which was supported by a carefully planned marketing strategy, paid off. By 1993, the Nintendo Company of America was selling six hundred thousand games and game-players per day.

Leadership

Without leadership, a good innovation goes nowhere. In 1970, Xerox founded the Palo Alto Research Center—to create the "office of the future." The team of research and development specialists developed the first PC—with a mouse, icons, and pull-down menus, as well as the first laser printer. But they were unable to commercialize these technologies into consumer products. That's because Xerox lacked the visionary leadership to look beyond the office copier business. According to Rogers, Xerox leaders also failed to implement mechanisms to transfer the technology developed at Palo Alto to the company's manufacturing and marketing divisions.

Steve Jobs, who had visited the Palo Alto operation in 1979, hired several of the center's employees and gave them his full support as they incorporated the technologies they had developed into the Macintosh computer, which was introduced in 1984.

As these five examples suggest, innovations don't just happen. They often occur only after visionary leaders carefully analyze the technology, resources, structure, and timing required to launch and sustain them.

EVALUATING INNOVATION

It doesn't take much to recognize God's innovative touch: buds on a tree in early spring, flowers bursting into bloom, a spectacular sunrise, majestic mountains arching toward the sky. We also see the results of innovation all around us at work: technological advances ranging from computers to cell phones to the Internet. Yes, these innovations came about through human ideas, but where did these ideas come from? Originally, they came from God.

Use the following questions to evaluate what you have just read about innovation and then consider what your own feelings are about creativity in the workplace. Be sure to share your thoughts with at least one other person.

1. WHAT IS THE MOST INNOVATIVE THING YOU HAVE SEEN RECENTLY WHERE YOU WORK?

   Why did this innovation impress you? What difference has it made so far? Was this innovation immediately embraced by all who would be affected by it? Why or why not?

2. HOW WOULD YOU RATE YOURSELF AS AN INNOVATOR?

   Do you like to be involved in things that are new and fresh? Or do you prefer to just learn how things are and how they operate effectively, and then just leave them that way?

3. DO YOU THINK THERE ARE TIMES WHEN INNOVATION SHOULD BE SQUELCHED? IF SO, UNDER WHAT CIRCUMSTANCES? IN SITUATIONS THAT YOU FEEL CALL FOR INNOVATION, WHAT IS THE BEST WAY TO ENCOURAGE IT?

   Before reading this chapter, had you ever thought of God as being "innovative"? As followers of Christ, what should our attitude be toward innovation, especially in the workplace? Why should we have this attitude?

PRAYING *About* INNOVATION

Without a doubt, some people are naturally more innovative than others, but the Scriptures assure us that as creations of God in His image, we all share in His creative nature to some degree. Consider the following prayer to help you talk with Him about how you can use your innovative abilities to enhance your environment and influence those around you.

God, You are indeed the Master Innovator and I thank you for giving us some of Your creative qualities. Where would we be today without innovators like Alexander Graham Bell, Jonas Salk, Henry Ford, and so many others? I may never develop an innovation of their magnitude, but I know that I can use the creativity instilled in me to make a difference in my job, my company, and the people in it. Open my eyes to new ideas and enable me to avoid clinging to comfortable but outdated systems and practices.

Recommended Resources on Innovation

Beyond Words, by Ron DiCianni, Tyndale Press, 1998.
Circle of Innovation, by Tom Peters, Knopf, 1997.
Creating Mind, by Howard E. Gardner, Basic Books, 1994.
The Creative Priority, by Jerry Hirshberg, HarperBusiness, 1998.
Creativity in Business, by Michael Ray and Rochelle Myers, Doubleday, 1986.
deBono's Thinking Course, by Edward deBono, Facts on File Inc., 1982.
Innovation and Entrepreneurship: Practice and Principles, by Peter Drucker, Harper-Business, 1993.
Jamming, by John Kao, HarperBusiness, 1996.
A Whack on the Side of the Head, by Roger Von Oech, Warner Books, 1983.

13

The Spirit of Entrepreneurship

To look at Stan's résumé, you might think that he was one of those people who can't hold a job. After all, he had been with seventeen companies over twenty-three years. Except he had been president and a founding partner of each one, and none of them had gone bankrupt. In fact, the businesses had charted a consistent pattern of success, even though Stan remained directly involved with only two of them.

"I start them—you sustain them" was his personal motto. Stan enjoyed the thrill of the chase, the challenge of seeing an exciting idea take shape and then become reality. However, once the venture became established, he quickly grew bored and began looking for something else to do. You could almost predict when that time would come—the bounce in his step was not quite so high, the sparkle in his eyes was a little dimmer, and he seemed a bit impatient with tasks that seemed to energize him just weeks before.

One day, he was being interviewed by a college student who was doing a graduate research paper on entrepreneurship. The conversation helped Stan put into words some thoughts that had been going through his mind for some time.

"You know, there was a time when I thought something was wrong with me," Stan confided. "People all around me seemed content with keeping a daily routine, performing predictable jobs for equally predictable financial rewards. I was more like the explorer who felt drawn to the mountains on the horizon, wondering what was on the other side.

When I got to the other side, I discovered that there was another mountain, and I wondered what was on the other side of it! One day, I just decided that predictable is okay—for some people—but there are others, like me, whose lot in life is always to find out what's on the other side of the next mountain."

Stan explained that he did not think that people who carried on what he had started were any less talented or creative. In fact, he acknowledged that if it were not for people like them, none of the businesses he started would remain in existence. "And it takes talent and creativity to keep a business going, handling normal, day-to-day issues and dealing with changes and obstacles as they arise," he said. "Unlike explorers, these men and women are more like settlers, the people who studied the land that had been taken and were willing to do the hard work of building the area into something special and then sustaining it. But some people are just born to be entrepreneurs. They move ahead, getting new things started, and then they move on once the novelty starts to wear off. I guess some people are called to live according to an entrepreneurial spirit and others aren't. Neither type is better than the other; they're just different."

■ ■

By any measure, entrepreneurship is on the rise. The number of new businesses continues to reach record levels, partly because of the number of business and professional people who have found it necessary to start a company after taking early retirement or after being victimized by their employer's downsizing. Others, weary of the corporate grind, choose to take the entrepreneurial route so that they can finally work on their own terms—doing what they want, when they want to do it. Statistics confirm this migration to start-ups. For example, a 1997 study shows that 885,416 new employer firms were established in the United States that year. That total, the highest ever at that point, was a 5.1 percent increase over the previous record, which was set just the year before. Over a broader time frame, the number of small businesses in the United States—at least one indication of entrepreneurial activity—has increased by 57 percent since 1982.

This escalation of interest in entrepreneurial activity shows no sign of going away. According to both anecdotal feedback and hard research, more men and women than ever before anticipate engaging in entrepreneurial pursuits at some point as they travel toward their career horizon.

The word *entrepreneur* can be used either as a noun or as an adjective. To say, "I am an entrepreneur" indicates a formal role or job description. It is a designation that people carry with themselves to their work. But to use the word as an adjective and assert, "I am entrepreneurial" suggests an approach to work rather than an official title.

As usual, Peter Drucker cuts to the core of the issue. "An entrepreneur," he said in a 1996 interview with *Inc.* magazine, "is someone who gets something new done." Getting something new done can happen in virtually any professional context. An entrepreneurial spirit permeates the thinking and action of a new enterprise as it gets off the ground. And that same spirit can fuel the approach of an individual in a large corporate environment.

Whether working in a start-up or in a centuries-old corporation, an entrepreneur looks at life very differently from his nonentrepreneurial colleagues. According to Howard Stevenson and David Gumpert (*Harvard Business Review,* March–April 1985), the difference in perspective can be characterized by the kinds of questions asked in evaluating opportunities.

The typical administrator asks:

- What resources do I control?
- What structure determines our organization's relationship to its market?
- How can I minimize the impact of others on my ability to perform?
- What opportunity is appropriate?

In contrast, the entrepreneur asks:

- Where is the opportunity?
- How do I capitalize on it?
- What resources do I need?
- How do I gain control over them?
- What structure is best?

Being an entrepreneur has most to do with one's approach to work. The Old Testament patriarch Abraham, for example, was an entrepreneur. He lived in the ancient Mesopotamian city of Ur around 2000 B.C. At age seventy-five, this successful businessman was called by God to leave Ur and begin his professional life all over again in a foreign land.

Archeological excavations that took place in the mid-twentieth century revealed that Ur had had a population of around one million. More significant from a business point of view, Ur was the world's cultural and trade crossroad of its day. It even boasted massive structures, each serving as a center for international commerce. So Abraham left a sophisticated city with a thriving business community when he headed off to a relatively undeveloped and rural land that had no such commercial infrastructure.

To paraphrase Drucker, Abraham had to get something new done. And he did—building another very successful enterprise. The biblical accounts that track his progress (Genesis 11:27–25:10 and Hebrews 11:8–19) leave us with four characteristics that, taken together, define the spirit of entrepreneurship: (1) calling mixed with destiny, (2) transition mixed with flexibility, (3) hope mixed with faith, and (4) creativity mixed with independence. First, we'll look at the passage from Hebrews, and then we'll discuss the four characteristics, which the passage presents.

> Now faith is being sure of what we hope for and certain of what we do not see. . . . By faith Abraham, when called to go to a place he would later receive as his inheritance, obeyed and went, even though he did not know where he was going. By faith he made his home in the promised land like a stranger in a foreign country; he lived in tents, as did Isaac and Jacob, who were heirs with him of the same promise. For he was looking forward to the city with foundations, whose architect and builder is God. All these people were still living by faith when they died. They did not receive the things promised; they only saw them and welcomed them from a distance. And they admitted that they were aliens and strangers on earth. People who say such things show that they are looking for a country of their own. If they had been thinking of the coun-

try they had left, they would have had opportunity to return. Instead, they were longing for a better country—a heavenly one. Therefore God is not ashamed to be called their God, for he has prepared a city for them. By faith Abraham, when God tested him, offered Isaac as a sacrifice. He who had received the promises was about to sacrifice his one and only son, even though God had said to him, "It is through Isaac that your offspring will be reckoned." Abraham reasoned that God could raise the dead, and figuratively speaking, he did receive Isaac back from death (Hebrews 11:1, 8–19).

CALLING MIXED *with* DESTINY

There can be no misunderstanding regarding how Abraham became an entrepreneur. God called him to be one. Genesis 12:1 and Hebrews 11:8 make it clear that because God called, the only appropriate response was for Abraham to obey. And he did so with dispatch. According to the verb tenses in the original languages of the biblical text, as God was calling, Abraham was packing. As God was talking, Abraham's feet were moving. There was no hesitation.

Entrepreneurs are frontline folks who are obsessed with the concept of calling and destiny. There is an inner compulsion, a pull from the heart that compels them to work around the clock, against incredible resistance and in the face of obvious logic. What could possibly make a successful, secure executive walk away from a stable corporate life to go and do a new thing? Often, an inner sense of calling and destiny is the only answer.

Not only do entrepreneurs feel called, but they also have what seem to be grandiose visions of the future. Abraham was willing to live in a tent on a barren hillside. But what did he see in his mind's eye? He was looking forward to a city (Hebrews 11:10). Abraham did not sit outside his tent in the cool night air and dream about building a house. No, he visualized an entire city.

Magellan was the first human to circumnavigate the globe. He was forever peering out from the boat he was on toward the horizon that was before him. According to Os Guiness, in his book *The Call* (W Publishing, 1998), "Magellan was a dreamer fired by intervention and fortified by devout faith which made him in the words of his fellow captains, tough, tough, tough." No matter what happened, Magellan's response was always, "Sail on, sail on, sail on." His sailors were emaciated, all the food stores were exhausted, the sails were rotting, the riggings were tattered, and the sun was merciless, but he never flinched. He was gripped by a sense of destiny and calling.

Entrepreneurs often do the illogical. Their friends and family members many times think they are crazy. But what looks unreasonable, unwise, and uncomfortable from the outside all makes sense to the entrepreneur. The biblical text does not record the responses of Abraham's friends to his announcement that he would be leaving town and beginning business and life elsewhere. But it would not be difficult to write the script.

The prime motivation for an entrepreneur's effort must be her calling. She responds to the drumbeat of destiny, to the sense of internal mandate coming from a divine calling that has settled in her soul. Abraham really had no choice. He was called to be an entrepreneur.

Transition Mixed *with* Flexibility

Founders of a hundred companies interviewed by *Inc.* magazine in 1989 revealed that entrepreneurs gave little priority to their initial business plans. Forty-one percent had no business plan, 26 percent wrote theirs on the back of an envelope, and just 5 percent worked up financial projections for investors. Only 28 percent wrote a full-blown business plan. According to the survey, most entrepreneurs don't bother with significant strategic planning, because they thrive in rapidly changing business environments that tend to scare away existing companies. Flexibility is the key.

When Abraham left his home, he didn't know where he was going or when he would get there—and that seemed to be okay with him. In the words of Genesis 12:1, God said to Abraham, "Leave your country . . . and go to the land I will show you." Hebrews 11:8 comments that Abraham "obeyed and went even though he did not know where he was going." There is nothing in the text to suggest that an arrangement based on uncertainty was a burden to Abraham.

Entrepreneurs are people who are going somewhere but who are not exactly sure where they will end up. That does not mean that they don't have a mission or a well-defined sense of direction. It does mean, however, that the road to the destination most likely will not be level and straight; it will be filled with unexpected hills and turns.

Flexibility and transition are key innate components in the life of an entrepreneur. Unanswered questions and uncertainty in professional life might bother many, but they are understood as necessary components of an entrepreneur's professional existence. And entrepreneurs can't live without ambiguity.

Typically, entrepreneurs juggle too many balls at one time, and they can drive other people crazy. Observers wonder, "Why can't they just stick to one thing?" It's not really a factor of personality; rather, it's how these venturesome business people are wired inside. They are terrified by the constant; they are energized by the unknown.

Years ago, we were meeting with the CEO of a potential client company. The CEO was considering hiring us as consultants to the company, so he asked us to interact with the principals of his business. It was an established, successful, maturing industrial company, and the leaders were thinking about starting another company in a related field. From the start, it was evident that the CEO had a very strong entrepreneurial bent that was driving the expansion plans.

Some months later, we returned for a follow-up discussion concerning our consultation services. We were amazed at what had transpired during the time in between. The parent company had grown to more than twice the size it was when we were there the first time, through the acquisition of two other companies. The CEO had led the charge in starting two other regional companies, and now the staff was actively researching the start of two franchising opportunities that could be prototyped and then expanded around the country. All of this had taken place within less than one year.

HOPE MIXED *with* FAITH

Real entrepreneurs have the makings of good theologians, since much of what they do equates to acts of faith. Business literature defines entrepreneurs as those who "take risks." In contrast, scripture requires that an entrepreneur "have faith." Faith in whom? Themselves? No. Faith in God. Hebrews 11:1, by way of introduction to Abraham and other Old Testament heroes, states it this way: "Now faith is being sure of what we hope for and certain of what we do not see." Such faith acts as the catalyst that brings the dreams and visions of the entrepreneur into reality.

One of the most distinguishing characteristics of an entrepreneur is the ability to look into the future and see something that does not currently exist. Furthermore, entrepreneurs have genuine confidence that their visions can become reality.

Not all leaps into the unknown are statements of faith. Sometimes, entrepreneurial high risk is wrongly fueled by stilted optimistic presumption. Manly Beasley (one of Steve Graves's mentors) loved to tell the story of the impulsive apostle Peter jumping out of the boat to go see Jesus. He was able to walk on the water because Jesus called him, not because he willed himself to do so. Real faith is always directed by an invitation from Jesus. Both Peter and Abraham had that invitation—and responded accordingly.

Real faith is not something manufactured from deep within by an individual's drive, adventurousness, or curiosity. It is only possible when it is directed by an invitation from Christ. Faith is the ability to trust God so as to do what He calls us to do.

According to scripture, entrepreneurs who live in this world of hope and faith are willing to live with less reward now, in anticipation of greater reward in the future (Hebrews 11:9b-10a). In addition, they refuse to look back and second-guess the path they have chosen. In fact, the text makes it clear that "if they had been thinking of the country they had left, they would have had opportunity to return" (Hebrews 11:15). An entrepreneur's life is not easy. These individuals do not use the rearview mirror. Without the look forward, it is too easy to turn back.

CREATIVITY MIXED *with* INDEPENDENCE

Entrepreneurs clear their own land. Like the pioneers who tamed the Wild West, entrepreneurs like to blaze fresh trails, unravel confounding mysteries, and explore uninhabited frontiers. Doing the same thing over and over again is not their definition of a good day. Telling entrepreneurs that an idea will not fly only makes them more determined to pull it off.

God wired Abraham in such a way that the patriarch thrived on the challenge of figuring out how to make business work. Instead of remaining comfortable in the security of what *had been* successful, Abraham was called to go and do it over again—in a different place and in a different way. He was not content to live vicariously off another's set of experiences. He experienced life on his own.

In an established organizational context, entrepreneurs often show up as change agents or as individuals who attempt to accomplish the unusual outside normal channels. And that is a good thing. Drucker, in *Innovation and Entrepreneurship* (HarperBusiness, 1993), points out that entrepreneurial activity—which any organization must engage in to survive—must be nurtured separately from the existing structure if it is to be successful.

It is not surprising that a majority of start-up businesses fail. There are real and hidden dangers to clearing uninhabited land. You don't know what you don't know. But neither is it surprising that, in the face of discouraging data, entrepreneurs try new ventures anyway. Their creativity and desire for a measure of independence drives them to do so.

A MODERN-DAY ENTREPRENEURIAL EXAMPLE

Gordon Addington (Tom Addington's father) is an entrepreneur. He gets new things done, which he has succeeded at all his life. He can't help it; that is how God wired him. While in the midst of his seminary education, he planted a church. After deciding that God was calling him and his young family to overseas mission work, he completed a medical degree and moved to Hong Kong. His intention was to open an outpatient clinic, but he ended up building a hospital instead. He is now in his seventies, and he continues to blaze new trails. A man of deep faith in Jesus, he has never been uncertain of his call.

He embodies, as well as anybody, the characteristics of the entrepreneurial spirit evidenced in Abraham. Throughout his life, Gordon has been a pioneer. He has always marched to the beat of a different drummer—a beat that can be heard only in the heart of an entrepreneur.

At the end of their career, entrepreneurs sit on their porch and say, "That was some ride!"—which a lot of teens say after experiencing an incredible roller coaster ride. Completing something new has its ups and downs, but it always leaves someone who is called to be an entrepreneur with a magnificent sense of satisfaction and contentment.

EVALUATING ENTREPRENEURSHIP

Some people can be classified as *pioneers,* meaning that they always like to be involved in something new—and then grow tired of it, no matter how successful it is, when it starts to seem a little old. Others can be termed *settlers,* signifying that they thrive on taking on something that has an established, sure course and sticking with it, maintaining and developing it to its fullest potential. Not everyone is wired to be an entrepreneur, and if we all were entrepreneurs, who would keep things going once the novelty turned to routine? To help you determine where you fall on the entrepreneurial spectrum, get with a friend or with a small group of people and discuss your responses to the following questions:

1. IN AN ESTABLISHED ORGANIZATIONAL CONTEXT, ENTREPRENEURS OFTEN SHOW UP AS CHANGE AGENTS OR AS INDIVIDUALS WHO ATTEMPT TO ACCOMPLISH THE UNUSUAL OUTSIDE NORMAL CHANNELS. DO YOU AGREE WITH THIS STATEMENT? WHY OR WHY NOT?

    What is it about organizational structures that can impede change or the accomplishment of the unusual? Does it have to be this way?

2. IN YOUR VIEW, HOW MUCH DOES FAITH HAVE TO DO WITH STEPPING OUT AND TAKING A RISK IN AN ENTREPRENEURIAL ENTERPRISE? DOES THIS FAITH COME FROM GOD, OR DOES IT COME FROM SOME OTHER SOURCE?

    Obviously, not all entrepreneurs are followers of Christ, just as not all followers of Christ are entrepreneurs. But to what extent do you think trusting in Jesus is like being an entrepreneur in business?

3. ON A SCALE FROM 1 TO 10 (1 BEING "NOT AT ALL" AND 10 BEING "EXTREMELY SO"), HOW WOULD YOU RATE YOUR INCLINATION TOWARD ENTREPRENEURSHIP? EXPLAIN YOUR ANSWER.

    If you are not strongly entrepreneurial by nature, can you think of any areas in your life where it might be helpful to be more willing to step out and take a risk? And if you are strongly entrepreneurial, can you see areas of your life where it might be advisable to proceed more cautiously than your natural inclination would lead you to do?

Praying *About* Entrepreneurship

Whether God has wired you to be entrepreneurial or not, there is no need to feel either prideful or apologetic. An entrepreneur has been called to be so, just as the person who functions best in a secure, established environment has been called to work in that manner. But there are times when the Lord calls us to step out in faith and take risks based on our trust in Him, even those of us who don't register the smallest blip on the entrepreneurial scale. Let the following prayer guide you as you examine what God might want to tell you about this area of entrepreneurship.

God, I thank you for the spirit of entrepreneurship, especially as shown by biblical patriarchs who today serve as examples of stepping out in faith and following the path You had chosen for them, even when their destinations were unclear or unknown, and who have blazed trails for us to follow. And I thank you for the knowledge that following You is perhaps the grandest entrepreneurial venture of all, for what You desire to do through me to make a difference in the world.

Recommended Resources on Entrepreneurship

The E-Myth: Why Most Small Businesses Don't Work and What to Do About It, by Michael Gerber, Ballinger, 1985.

The Entrepreneurial Venture, by William A. Sahlman and Howard H. Stevenson (editors), Harvard Business School Press, 1992.

How to Succeed in Business by Breaking All the Rules: A Plan for Entrepreneurs, by Dan S. Kennedy and Scott Degarmo, Plume, 1997.

Innovation and Entrepreneurship: Practice and Principles, by Peter Drucker, HarperBusiness, 1993.

Small Time Operator: How to Start Your Own Small Business, Keep Your Books, Pay Your Taxes and Stay Out of Trouble! by Bernard B. Kamoroff, Bell Springs, 1998.

The Start-Up Entrepreneur: How You Can Succeed in Building Your Own Company, by James R. Cook, Plume, 1997.

Visionary Business: An Entrepreneur's Guide to Success, by Marc Allen, New World Library, 1997.

Marketplace Grace

Brenda would never have been mistaken for one of Emily's friends. As the heads of the marketing and accounting departments, respectively, for their company, they often took opposite sides on key decisions. Brenda felt that budgets and financial constraints were merely inventions by accounting practitioners to keep marketing staff people from working at marketing, whereas Emily always emphasized fiscal accountability and conservative spending. In addition, almost everyone knew how aggressively Brenda would lobby behind the scenes to undermine Emily's initiatives, sometimes even when they didn't have a direct effect on the marketing department.

Emily knew about Brenda's tactics, although she never understood why she insisted on being so adversarial. Twice she had asked to speak with Brenda to try to resolve their differences, but Brenda had no interest. She seemed to take delight in trying to make Emily's work—and life—as difficult as possible. Eventually, Emily stopped trying to make peace with her. "Brenda's going to do what she's going to do," she told one of her associates. "I'll just keep my distance and try to keep from responding to her in kind."

So the surprise on Brenda's face was understandable that terrible evening at the hospital, after her teenaged son had been seriously injured in a car accident. A single mom, she was sitting alone at her son's bedside, feeling helpless and struggling to comprehend what the future might hold for them both. Then the door opened—and Emily walked in.

Walking directly to Brenda and placing a hand lightly on her shoulder, Emily simply said, "I thought you might need a friend." Then she sat down and with hardly a word, listened as Brenda poured out her heart, explaining what she understood about the accident and the prognosis for her son. Staring into Emily's eyes, Brenda expected to see at least a hint of animosity, but she found none. She found instead only compassion and understanding.

The two women talked almost like long-lost sisters, and before they knew it, two hours had gone by. The boy's condition had not changed, but Brenda's heart had. In her mind, she recalled the many times she had consciously tried to thwart the plans of this kind woman sitting next to her—and could no longer understand what had motivated her to act so unfairly.

At about that time, Emily glanced at her watch and said, "Oh, I didn't realize it was getting so late. I have to go. But I'll be back tomorrow afternoon. Is there anything I can do for you?"

Brenda couldn't believe what she was hearing. "Thank you for coming—but why? After all I have done to you, I can't even give you a good reason for it. Why did you come? You didn't have to."

"I know," Emily replied with a bit of a smile. "But quite a while ago someone showed me a lot of grace, and it's the least I can do for you."

"Grace? I don't understand. And who showed it to you?"

"Let's talk about that tomorrow, okay?" Emily said, giving Brenda one more hug before she left.

■ ■

Confusion overcame the young boy as he stood at a distance and watched his grandfather kneel before a tombstone. It was the end of a long day, and he hadn't understood everything he'd seen. Conversations, when they took place at all, were whispered. Information and insights were in short supply.

But he had an idea for solving the problem. When the time was right, he would ask. And if that didn't work, he would ask again. And again. He was a brave boy, and his courage allowed him to feed his curiosity when others might let theirs go hungry. So later that day the boy called upon that courage and climbed onto the lap of his grandfather.

"Granddad," he said, "Why did we go to that cemetery, and why did it make you cry?"

James Ryan looked into the eyes of his grandson and saw compassion as well as curiosity. What would become of this boy? Ryan wondered. And what of his children and their children? What differences would they make in the world?

The boy needed the answer to his questions, but not just to satisfy his curiosity. The answer was profound, something that might change the boy's life. "We owe our lives to the man who was buried in that grave," Ryan said. "Without him, I wouldn't be here. Your father wouldn't be here. And you wouldn't be here."

"What did the man do?" the boy asked.

"He saved Private Ryan."

GRACE *in the* MARKETPLACE

Steven Spielberg might not fully understand the grace of Christ, but he understands the concept of grace. The theme runs deep in many of the fifty-plus movies directed and/or produced by the Jewish filmmaker—most notably in *Schindler's List* (1993), *Amistad* (1997), and *Saving Private Ryan* (1998).

Grace is a powerful element of storytelling because grace is a powerful connector between God and people. It transcends human understanding and brings the spiritual into play. It opens the portal for seeing, feeling, and experiencing the life-changing love of God, but in ways that often are worked out through people.

Amazing grace, indeed.

Grace is the goodness of God extended to us that we do not deserve and can never repay. Furthermore, it's a goodness that we, as followers of Christ, can then extend to others.

In the context of the marketplace, the extension of that grace remains as important as ever. Why? Because in its fullness, marketplace grace is a concept often trampled under the stampede of misguided ethics, cutthroat competition, outright illegalities, fierce office politics, unbridled arrogance, uncontrollable circumstances, and out-and-out evil.

Some argue that grace has no place in the free market. On the contrary, Grace was created precisely for such a time as this.

In *Saving Private Ryan,* James Ryan began to understand grace when a small group of soldiers hunted him down with orders to take

him out of harm's way. Even when he learned the Army's reasoning—
that his three brothers had been killed in action and that the Army
wanted to spare his mother the heartache of losing all four of her sons
in the war, Ryan's sense of duty and fairness compelled him to stay for
one final battle.

Later, as the captain who found Ryan lay dying of battle wounds,
he looked at Ryan and said, "Earn this." It was an impossible request,
but one that Ryan, moviegoers can infer, must have spent the rest of
his life trying to fulfill. Not everyone responds to this challenge, however—especially in the marketplace.

In the parable of the unmerciful servant (Matthew 18:21–35), a
king decides to settle all of his accounts. A servant who can't pay his
debts begs for mercy, promising that in time he will pay. "The servant's
master took pity on him, canceled the debt and let him go" (verse 27).

The servant then comes upon someone who owes him money.
That person can't pay, so the servant has him thrown into prison.
When the master finds out, he calls in the servant and chastises him
for not demonstrating the same grace that he had been shown. Then
he throws the servant into prison "to be tortured, until he should pay
back all he owed" (verse 34).

Notice two things about this parable. First, there's no "religious"
language. The purpose of the parable is not to show that in a marketplace setting grace should be preached. It's about an approach to
life; we need to live out a life of grace that is so different from what
others might expect or deserve that they cannot help but say, "That's
unbelievable."

Second, there's a harsh edge to the parable, found in verse 35:
"This is how my heavenly Father will treat each of you unless you forgive your brother from your heart." As followers of Christ, we are immersed in grace. If we refuse to give grace, our lives will be miserable.

GRACE *in the* COURT *of a* KING

What is marketplace grace, and how do we live it out? What does it
look like? How is it demonstrated in such times as this?

We found some answers in another story, one that very likely was
told to a wide-eyed grandson by his Jewish grandfather several thousand years ago:

"Why are we honoring this woman?" the boy might have asked.

"She was the instrument God used to save His people," the grandfather responded. "Because of God's grace through her life, we are alive today."

Grace, because it involves God's good gifts to us, is often presented only in a positive light. But the story of Esther is a more full-orbed, complete picture than that. The grace in Esther is grace that stands against pure evil. It stands against huge ego and arrogance. It stands against people. It stands against injustice. The grace story of Esther is a story of winners and losers, not just winners. Some are granted life, and some have life taken away.

Marketplace grace as we experience it today seldom results in life or death outcomes, but it's certainly the kind where there are winners and losers—just as there were with Esther.

Esther's story is set in the Persian city of Susa, between 485 and 465 B.C., during the reign of Xerxes I. It was Xerxes's son, Artaxerxes, who allowed Ezra and Nehemiah to do their part in the rebuilding of Jerusalem and the Jews' return from exile. But the way for that to occur first had to be made possible by the grace of God demonstrated through Esther.

Xerxes conducted a Cinderella-like search for a queen and picked Esther, not knowing she was Jewish. She had been adopted by her cousin, Mordecai, a man apparently of high stature in the Jewish community who, whenever possible, continued to advise her even after she became queen.

Haman, who rose to power in the court of Xerxes, had it in for Mordecai because Mordecai refused to kneel before him. Rather than take his anger out on Mordecai alone, Haman persuaded the king to issue an edict setting aside a specific day for the annihilation of all the Jews throughout every one of the royal provinces. When Mordecai learned of this, he sent word to his cousin, Queen Esther, seeking her help.

Understandably, Esther was reluctant. It was illegal to approach the king without being summoned. If Esther did so and the king wasn't happy to see her, she would be killed. But Mordecai didn't drop his challenge; he increased it. If she didn't help, he predicted, God would find another way to deliver the Jews, and her family would come to ruin. "And who knows but that you have come to royal position for such a time as this?" (Esther 4:14).

Esther rose to the challenge. She took the risk and went to the king, who received her with favor. When he asked what he could do for her, she simply asked that he and Haman dine with her that day. During dinner, the king again asked her what she wanted. So she asked the king and Haman to have dinner with her again the next night.

This time, when the king asked her what she wanted, Esther dropped the bomb. She asked Xerxes to protect her people, and she exposed Haman's evil for what it was. Haman ended up hanged on the very gallows he had ordered built for Mordecai.

Xerxes, by the law of the culture, couldn't reverse his edict, so he issued a new proclamation allowing the Jews to defend themselves. In doing so, they defeated seventy-five thousand of their enemies. And Mordecai, who had demonstrated his loyalty to the king, rose in rank second only to Xerxes himself.

PRINCIPLES *for* OUR TIMES

It's unlikely that any of us will soon find ourselves in Esther's position, but the modern marketplace overflows with dilemmas similar to those that she faced. We work with people who are arrogant or downright evil. We find ourselves challenged to stand against injustices. Our faith—and sometimes our careers—become tested by our ability to tactfully uphold our values.

As we examined the story of Esther, we identified these lessons for living out marketplace grace in the modern work world:

1.   GRACE SHINES BRIGHTEST AMID EVIL'S DARKNESS.

Haman's plot (Esther 3:8–15) represents the skillful manipulation of the king for purely evil purposes: the destruction of the Jewish race.

Needless to say, word of the king's edict was of great concern to the Jews. Without grace, they would be killed, and there was little they could do about it. Grace, of course, is present in every context; but in great darkness, even a small amount of light makes a tremendous difference because there's such a huge contrast. God's grace was seen in Esther, and the story of how God rescued His people became a beacon of hope to future generations.

2. GRACE REQUIRES BACKBONE AND INVOLVES RISK, OFTEN IN THE
   FACE OF INJUSTICE.

Esther risked that the king might kill her simply because she approached him without an invitation. Furthermore, it was almost certain that Xerxes would discover her ethnicity. So if the king let his order stand, she would die along with the other Jews.

In the marketplace, followers of Christ sometimes back away from confrontation, and sometimes they do so in the name of grace. Grace doesn't mean we never challenge injustice; it means we do it in a certain graceful way. Certainly, Xerxes would have scored Esther as maneuvering in a graceful way.

3. GOD USES HIS PEOPLE AS AGENTS OF HIS GRACE.

Grace is delivered from God. And while it's not always the case, often people serve as His agents. Jesus, the best example, is the agent of God's grace, and He came in person to deliver it.

God chose to use Esther as the way to solve the problem created by Haman. In an environment that longed for God's grace, Esther became the vehicle—the agent of grace attitudes and grace movements, the agent of a gracious lifestyle.

Furthermore, grace is a concept that's bigger than personality types. Most of us know people who are more gracious and more graceful than others. It's part of who they are. Esther, besides being in the right place at the right time, was known for her physical beauty, and she obviously had an inviting personality. But the call for living out grace in the marketplace is a call to everyone, and it's bigger than our personal wiring. Wiring doesn't overpower God's grace.

4. GRACE IS MOST NEEDED WHEN THERE IS EXTRAORDINARY
   ARROGANCE.

Haman had no idea that Esther was putting together her banquets to expose him. In fact, he felt honored as the only one other than the king whom the queen had invited. He left work in a great mood—until he passed the king's gates and saw Mordecai, the man who refused to bow before him. When he got home, he gathered his wife and friends and "boasted to them about his vast wealth, his many sons, and all the ways the king had honored him" (Esther 5:11). When he complained about Mordecai, his wife and friends suggested that he have gallows built so that Mordecai could be hanged on them, and that's what he did.

Haman showed no regard for anyone other than himself. He was so self-agenda driven that he was willing to use anyone and everyone for his own personal purposes. We don't know the hearts of other people, but the expression of their activities shows whether they have anyone's interest involved other than their own. Haman didn't. He woke up and went to bed totally focused on one person—himself.

Arrogance is among the most present problems in the workplace today. It produces a huge need for grace. But grace didn't mean that Esther ignored the arrogance or that we should. It requires that we be strategic in our thinking and that we adhere to a process that honors God.

5.   GOD'S SOVEREIGNTY IS EVIDENT IN AN ENVIRONMENT OF GRACE.

Sometimes, it's easy to think that our part in a situation is central to the outcome, forgetting that God is at work in a bigger way. Even though God was not mentioned once in the book of Esther, clearly God controlled the drama.

Not long after Esther was made queen, for instance, Mordecai was sitting near the king's gates. He overheard two men, who guarded the king's doorway, plotting to kill Xerxes. Mordecai told Esther, who credited Mordecai when she told the king. The conspirators were discovered and executed, and Mordecai's loyalty was recorded in the annals (Esther 2:21–23).

Skip ahead to the night before Esther's second banquet. Haman had ordered gallows built just so he could see Mordecai swing from them. But that night, Xerxes suffered from insomnia and asked for the best sleeping pill he knew of—a reading from the book of the annals. When the account of Mordecai's loyalty was read, the king wondered whether anything had been done to honor the man who saved the king's life. Nothing, he was told.

At this time, Haman waited in the outer courts for an opportunity to talk to the king about hanging Mordecai. The king called him in and said, "What should be done for the man the king delights to honor?" Haman, in his arrogance, assumed the king planned to honor him, so he said such a man should be led through the city wearing one of the king's robes and riding one of the king's horses. And, he said, a noble prince should lead the way, proclaiming to all that this is how the king treats those who delight him. Great idea, Xerxes said. I want you to do just that for Mordecai.

God's sovereignty here—His rebuke of the author of evil—would be ironic and almost humorous, were it not for the gravity of the situation.

6. GRACE INVOLVES STRATEGIC THINKING AND ACTION.

When Esther decided to help her people, she didn't rush right off to wake the king and beg for his mercy, nor did she threaten him with verses from scripture. She prayed and fasted, and she asked others to pray and fast on her behalf. Then she came up with a well-thought-out plan.

Sometimes, we think of grace as a random occurrence. Because God is the author, we think we don't have much to do with it; it is our notion that our part is not central to the outcome. That was certainly not true in Esther's case. She was heavily involved in putting her brain to work, often without the help of other people.

We also often wrongly assume that we need to force God into the picture. But grace often is better expressed in social good deeds and social graces than with religious language and religious activity—especially in the marketplace. Again, God isn't directly mentioned in the story of Esther, but a huge work both by God and for God was done.

7. GRACE INCLUDES WINNERS AND LOSERS.

The winners and losers couldn't have been contrasted more strikingly in this case. Haman and all of his sons were put to death. The Jews defeated their enemies. And Mordecai became the equivalent of the kingdom's prime minister—the second most powerful person in the land.

But it's important to remember that we don't know the full effects of grace until the last chapter is written. We get to read the last chapter of Esther. More often than not, when we demonstrate grace in a marketplace situation, we don't get to see the end for a while, if at all. Esther had an inner sense of peace about pursuing the actions she felt called upon to take and then leaving the results to God. "I will go to the king, even though it is against the law," she said. "And if I perish, I perish" (Esther 4:16).

Most of us know people who have extended marketplace grace and have not yet seen the results. Their story remains involved in the human drama. Their boss hasn't changed. They are still overlooked. The gossip still goes on. Until we get to the final chapter, none of us knows the outcome. But we know that God will make it right.

EVALUATING MARKETPLACE GRACE

Greed, avarice, pride, rivalry, scheming—and even revenge. We see each of these in abundance in today's marketplace. It is as true today as it has been through the centuries. But grace—where do we find it? This is certainly not a virtue trumpeted in many of the revered business schools. And it's not likely to be the cover story in any of the revered business periodicals. But isn't it greatly needed at such a time as this? Using the following questions, discuss with someone your observations about marketplace grace—and how well you are doing in practicing it.

1. CAN YOU THINK OF A GOOD EXAMPLE OF A TIME WHEN YOU SAW MARKETPLACE GRACE IN ACTION? HAS THERE BEEN A TIME WHEN YOU HAD AN OPPORTUNITY TO EXTEND SUCH GRACE YOURSELF? EXPLAIN.

    Why do you think grace is such an uncommon commodity in today's business world? Would you say that many people—perhaps even you—would equate grace with weakness or foolishness?

2. WHAT DO YOU THINK OF THE IDEA THAT GRACE INVOLVES WINNERS AND LOSERS? WHEN WE HEAR MESSAGES ABOUT BIBLICAL GRACE, DON'T THEY USUALLY COME TO US WITH A POSITIVE SLANT?

    How would you feel if you demonstrated or expressed grace to another person and that individual did not respond in kind? Would a negative response to your act of grace affect you adversely? Or, regardless of the response, would you be inclined to extend grace as readily at a future time?

3. THINK OF AN INSTANCE AT YOUR WORKPLACE WHERE A
   DEMONSTRATION OF BIBLICAL GRACE COULD MAKE A PROFOUND
   DIFFERENCE. WHO WOULD BE AFFECTED, AND WHAT DO YOU
   THINK THE EVENTUAL OUTCOME WOULD BE?

How—perhaps like Esther in the Old Testament—could God use you as an instrument of His grace where you work, or where you live? Do you think that with some strategic thinking and action, this could actually come about?

PRAYING *About* MARKETPLACE GRACE

The competition, the stress, and the ever-increasing pace of the marketplace seems hardly conducive to an atmosphere of grace, but when Jesus directs us to reflect His grace to the world around us, He includes no exceptions. But that may be good news. In an environment of "ungrace," true, God-generated grace can't be missed. And perhaps models of Christlike grace are what an unredeemed world needs to see the most. The following prayer may help you engage in some honest self-reflection on the perplexing topic of grace.

God, I know that one definition of grace is "unmerited favor," and I know that I did not merit the favor You showed me when you saved me from my sins and an eternity without you. I know I didn't—and still don't—deserve Your grace, but every day I work with people whom I consider especially undeserving of Your grace. I find it difficult to communicate or demonstrate grace to such selfish, uncaring, and ungracious people. I am grateful that You pour Your grace through me, as I lack the capacity in myself. Please teach me more about this amazing grace.

Recommended Resources on Marketplace Grace

Church on Sunday, Work on Monday, by Laura Nash and Scotty McLennan, Jossey-Bass, 2001.
Living Beyond the Daily Grind: Reflections on the Songs and Sayings in Scripture: Book I and Book II, by Charles R. Swindoll, W Publishing Group, 1988.
The Other Six Days: Vocation, Work, and Ministry in Biblical Perspective, by R. Paul Stevens, Regent College, 2000.
Roaring Lambs, by Bob Briner, Zondervan, 1993.
Transforming Your Workplace for Christ, by William Nix, Broadman & Holman, 1997.

What Kind of Legacy
Will *You* Leave Behind?

The church sanctuary was jammed and people still stood outside on the sidewalks, hoping to be able to squeeze in. Tears were in virtually every eye, but the tears of sadness were mingled with tears of joy. Yes, Coach Timmons had been an extremely successful football coach, having led his teams to hundreds of victories and half a dozen state championships. But it wasn't the big win over the archrival Central that everyone was thinking about, or the last-minute touchdown pass that vaulted the Eagles into the finals. All anyone could think about was Coach Timmons, the man.

Tommy had proudly agreed to be one of the pallbearers. He had been an all-state running back, but what he remembered about Coach Timmons was his insisting that Tommy master his chemistry class and that he not fall behind academically, even if it meant stepping away from the team. Tommy was so thankful, because when his injured knee ended his college career, he was still well prepared to pursue his college degree.

Rachel remembered the kind, compassionate thoughts Coach Timmons had conveyed to her when her father died unexpectedly during her sophomore year. He had even taken her aside at the funeral home and prayed for God to comfort her. She had been in one of his English classes and the coach had greeted her every morning with "How are you doing, Rachel?" He made it clear that he really wanted to know. In the years following, he had become like a second father to her.

As Mrs. Rodriguez thought about Coach Timmons, she thought of the time he and his wife showed up at her door, unannounced, with two huge bags of groceries. He had learned that as a single mother she was having a tremendous financial struggle. He said to her, "We just want to help." Since Mrs. Rodriguez's son, Juan, was a third-string lineman on the team, she knew that the gesture wasn't an attempt to protect one of the coach's star players.

Barry stared straight ahead, blinking to keep his tears from cascading down, as he recalled the hours Coach Timmons had spent with him, even though he had been a rebellious, disrespectful student who had developed far greater affection for alcohol and marijuana than anything the coach tried to teach him in class. Eventually, Coach Timmons's persistence and genuine care, long after everyone had given up, grabbed Barry's attention. The young man's life was never the same after that.

Nearly everyone in the pews—and those still standing outside—could have shared similar stories. The newspapers only knew the coach as a man who had achieved unparalleled success on the gridiron and had passed up many offers to coach at major colleges. But those who really knew him understood that he was an individual who had given extravagantly and unhesitatingly from his own life, knowing what God had promised: "I will give men in exchange for you, and people in exchange for your life" (Isaiah 43:4). It was a legacy that would not soon fade.

■ ■

A quiet residential street in Bentonville, Arkansas, is home to a nondescript municipal cemetery full of family burial plots, including some that date back a hundred years or more. Just inside one of the entrances lies a tombstone that likely would go unnoticed by anyone not looking for it. It's not particularly large, not particularly fancy. Closer inspection reveals a simple yet meaningful inscription: "Recipient of the Presidential Medal of Freedom."

The tombstone marks the grave of Wal-Mart founder Sam Walton, one of the most influential business personalities of the twentieth century. Walton was a consummate innovator, a shrewd competitor, and a maverick merchant. His ability to motivate his employees and engender their loyalty was legendary. But perhaps the best testament to his legacy is the fact that Wal-Mart, which grew into the country's largest retail chain on his watch, has expanded dramatically since his death in 1992. And with annual net sales that reached an all-time record of nearly $218 billion in 2001, its growth shows no sign of slowing.

Walton is remembered for his business acumen, but the epitaph on his tombstone says nothing about everyday low prices or Wal-Mart's state-of-the-art merchandise replenishment system. It doesn't mention that he was named "CEO of the Year" by the magazine *Financial World*, "Man of the Year" by *Retail Week*, and America's "Most Successful Merchant" by *Fortune*. Instead, it notes that he was the recipient of one of his country's highest civilian honors.

According to the citation, Walton received the Presidential Medal of Freedom because he was "a devoted family man, business leader, and statesman for democracy" who "embodies the entrepreneurial spirit and epitomizes the American dream." In other words, his epitaph says a great deal about his legacy.

That's often the case with epitaphs; they boil a lifetime of work, service, or character into a few words or phrases. But they rarely tell the whole story. That's because they're written from a human perspective, either by individuals before their death or by their grieving relatives after they're gone. Even people who lived less than an exemplary life can have nice words written on their tombstone. Consider this example at a Dallas cemetery: "As the flowers are all made sweeter by the sunshine and the dew, so this old world is made brighter by the lives of folks like you." The epitaph for a lovable grandmother? Guess again. Buried under this tombstone is none other than Bonnie Parker, half of the infamous bank-robbing duo known as Bonnie and Clyde.

From God's viewpoint, however, epitaphs (and the legacies they represent) look quite different. He doesn't look at one's life through rose-colored glasses. He sees it all—the good, the bad, the pretty, and the ugly. So from a heavenly perspective, one's epitaph doesn't come from a book of favorite quotes; it is determined by how one lived his or her life.

GOD'S SCORECARD

The words *epitaph* and *legacy* do not appear in the Bible. But God's view of legacy is evident throughout scripture, particularly in the historical record of the Old Testament kings.

The nation of Israel was formed as a theocracy, governed directly by God without the intervention of an earthly ruler. But during the time of the judges, the Israelites began to clamor for an earthly king so that they could be like other nations. God gave them what they wanted, even though it wasn't His best for them. The first three kings—Saul, David, and Solomon—ruled the twelve tribes of Israel as a united nation. But because Solomon turned away from God, the nation was split after he died, with the ten northern tribes forming the kingdom of Israel and the tribes of Judah and Benjamin forming the southern kingdom of Judah.

The kings took over the leadership of the Israelites from God, so it stands to reason that God was extremely interested in measuring their progress (or lack thereof) and in recording their legacies. This is evident in the sheer volume of material devoted to it; the Old Testament books of 1 and 2 Samuel, 1 and 2 Kings, and 1 and 2 Chronicles all track the activities of the Jewish kings. The story of each king includes an epitaph. The monarchs may have fought and won great battles, built great cities, and accumulated great wealth, but when their days were over, their legacies were summed up in one of two ways: they either did what was right in the eyes of the Lord or they did evil in the eyes of the Lord. (See Table 15.1 at the end of the chapter.)

By recording an epitaph for each king, God, in effect, was keeping a legacy scorecard. And as a whole, their record was nothing to be proud of: "In over 200 years of the northern kingdom's existence, *not one* of the 19 monarchs was godly," Charles R. Swindoll writes in *The Living Insights Study Bible* (Zondervan, 1996). "And in the more than 340 years of the southern kingdom's existence, *only eight* rulers walked with God, some of those inconsistently."

Every king was a mixture of good and bad, but in God's eyes, the legacies left by the kings were either good or evil. The record of each generation opened and closed with a statement that noted the king's name, the length of his reign, and whether he followed God. For example, Rehoboam, the first king of Judah, "did evil because he had not set his heart on seeking the Lord" (2 Chronicles 12:14). This pattern, which is repeated dozens of times, reveals that to God, a legacy is a value judgment. A businessman might earn a lot of money and accomplish great things for his company, but in the end, his eternal epitaph will reflect the answer to a single question: In all aspects of life—work, family, faith, finances, and so forth—did he do what was right in the eyes of God, or did he do evil in the eyes of God?

Although today's fast-paced business world may seem far removed from the ancient kingdom of Judah, many of the same legacy issues that faced the kings in those days still exist today. Think of Judah as a long-running business that was passed from one generation to the next not less than nineteen times. Some of the kings served God and left good legacies, only to have their successors ruin everything good they had built. Some left good legacies that were continued by their heirs. Others left evil legacies that spanned several generations. And a few inherited kingdoms that were barely surviving, only to turn things around by bringing the people's focus and devotion back to God.

"Judah, Inc." is what we might name a study in legacy that applies to everyone—from the CEO struggling to rebuild a company in the wake of an ethics scandal to the middle manager trying to develop a reputable department.

LESSONS *on* LEGACY

1. A GOOD LEGACY IS A PERSONAL CHOICE.

The fact that our predecessor left a good legacy does not guarantee that we will do the same. And we cannot force those who come after us to follow in our footsteps. It comes down to personal choice. At Judah, Inc., this was particularly noticeable in the father-son pair of Hezekiah and Manasseh. Herbert Lockyer notes in *All the Kings and Queens of the Bible* (Zondervan, 1961) that Hezekiah was more "unreservedly commended" than any other king of Judah, but his godly life didn't keep his son, Manasseh, from reviving all the abominations his father had destroyed. Manasseh *chose* to pursue evil.

Incidentally, the motivation that often drives the second generation away from a good legacy is an unhealthy spirit of independence. Surely, Manasseh had heard stories of how God had rescued his father's kingdom from Sennacherib, king of Assyria (2 Kings 18:17–19:37; 2 Chronicles 32:1–22). He also knew of his father's reputation: "There was no one like him among all the kings of Judah, either before him or after him" (2 Kings 18:5b). But instead of carrying on his father's godly heritage, Manasseh lived out the meaning of his name: *forgetting*. He had to do it his way. And his way definitely wasn't God's way.

Of course, while any one person can lose a good legacy, it's also true that any one person can break a bad cycle. But it's not easy. To overcome a bad legacy, we have to commit to getting rid of as many of the bad elements as possible—everything from corrupt business practices to sinful habits. That's what Josiah, Manasseh's grandson, did when he became king. "Under his direction, the altars of the Baals were torn down; he cut to pieces the incense altars that were above them, and smashed the Asherah poles, the idols and the images" (2 Chronicles 34:4). Just as Josiah made wholesale changes in the kingdom to ensure that godliness would be established once again, we also—if we've inherited a bad legacy in our business or family—must be willing to make drastic changes so that we can get back on the right track.

Getting rid of the bad elements often involves difficult personnel decisions. Asa, the third king of Judah, deposed his grandmother Maacah from her position as queen mother because of her stubborn idolatry (1 Kings 15:13). As Asa surely discovered, removing longtime associates from positions of power isn't easy, but it sometimes must be done.

Finally, it's worth noting that the influence of godly people doesn't end just because their successors may disregard their example and undo their good works. In fact, a solid legacy often serves as the inspiration for the rebirth of an organization, be it a company that's struggling for profitability, a football program that wants to climb back into the top ten, or a nation that's lost its focus on God.

Manasseh, who led Judah, Inc., for fifty-five years, left no stone unturned in his quest for wickedness. "He rebuilt the high places his father Hezekiah had destroyed; he also erected altars to Baal and made an Asherah pole, as Ahab king of Israel had done. . . . He sacrificed his own son in the fire, practiced sorcery and divination, and consulted mediums and spiritists" (2 Kings 21:3–6). But even Manasseh's destructive ways could not stamp out the legacy left by David—the only person in the Bible who is referred to as "a man after God's own heart." David set the standard when it came to godly legacies. He is often used as a reference in the kings' epitaphs, as in, "Asa did what was right in the eyes of the Lord, *as his father David had done"* (1 Kings 15:11, emphasis added).

David's godly legacy continued to have impact long after he was gone. There were periods of wickedness—extending for decades in Manasseh's case—but when a godly king returned to the throne, David's influence was still felt and heeded. This holds great hope for us, both in our professional life and in our personal life. There's little we can do to mandate anyone's behavior after we're gone, but that doesn't mean someone eventually won't refer back to our legacy and attempt to emulate it.

2. PRIDE IS A ROADBLOCK IN THE QUEST FOR A CHRIST-CENTERED LEGACY.

Even though several of the Jewish kings sought God wholeheartedly, they were still susceptible to the sin of pride. In more than one instance, this ugly disease put blemishes on legacies that were otherwise pure.

Uzziah, for example, was a great and godly builder during the first twenty years of his fifty-two-year reign, fortifying Jerusalem, strengthening Judah's military, and giving to his small country "extension and prosperity that it had not enjoyed since the days of Solomon," Lockyer writes. But as Uzziah's confidence grew and his fame spread, he lost his focus. "As far away as Egypt, people talked about him," Swindoll writes. "And then one day Uzziah began to believe what people were saying about him. . . . And that was precisely when he began his descent down the slippery slope of his own self-satisfaction. . . . In his stupid pride, Uzziah began to believe in himself rather than in God."

What happened next wasn't pretty. Wanting to emulate the kings of the east who exercised priestly as well as royal functions, Uzziah decided to enter the temple and offer incense on the golden altar. When a group of eighty-one priests confronted him, he angrily tried to proceed, but he was stopped in his tracks when God struck him with leprosy. And where did the king's sin get him? "Conscience-stricken because of his pride and disobedience, Uzziah hurriedly left the Temple to begin a life of loneliness," Lockyer writes. "From then on he had to live in a separate house assigned to lepers, isolated from society."

What a sad finale to a reign that began with such promise. And what a lesson to anyone in a leadership position: the best way to mar a good legacy is to allow pride to gain a foothold.

3.   ACHIEVEMENTS MEAN LITTLE IF A PERSON LACKS INTEGRITY.

Most of the Jewish kings probably organized great construction projects and fought successful battles against their enemies. But scripture generally records the accomplishments of only the good kings.

Jotham, the godly son of Uzziah, "rebuilt the Upper Gate of the temple of the Lord and did extensive work on the wall at the hill of Ophel. He built towns in the Judean hills and forts and towers in the wooded areas" (2 Chronicles 27:3–4). Hezekiah built storehouses for his vast collection of valuables. He also built villages and "blocked the upper outlet of the Gihon spring and channeled the water down to the west side of the City of David" (2 Chronicles 32:30). Asa, Jehoshaphat, Uzziah, and Josiah are also noted for their building achievements.

Their records are in stark contrast to Manasseh's story. He undoubtedly built *something* significant during his fifty-five-year reign, and 2 Chronicles 33:14–16 mentions some positive work he did after he repented near the end of his life. But the biblical record concentrates primarily on all the evil he perpetrated in the kingdom. Manasseh may have done some constructive things, but God seems preoccupied with his evil. When the time came to make a record of Manasseh's life (as well as the lives of the other wicked kings), the evil in his heart overshadowed his earthly accomplishments.

The historical account of the Jewish kings seems to suggest the following insight about leaving a legacy: when God finds people who demonstrate lives of integrity, He then moves to showcase their achievements. But if people lack integrity, their achievements are irrelevant. If we have an evil heart, the good things that we do mean nothing; at least, that is God's perspective of our legacy.

4.   GODLY MENTORS AND CHRIST-CENTERED RELATIONSHIPS ARE
     KEY TO BUILDING A GOOD LEGACY.

Relationships can make or break a legacy. This was abundantly clear at Judah, Inc. Jehoram, the fifth ruler of the southern kingdom, "walked in the ways of the kings of Israel, as the house of Ahab had done, for he married a daughter of Ahab" (2 Kings 8:18). Marrying into the family of one of the most wicked characters in all of scripture did nothing to enhance Jehoram's life. After his eight-year reign, 2 Chronicles 21:20 adds this sad note to his epitaph: "He passed away, *to no one's regret,* and was buried in the City of David" (emphasis added). How would you like to have that said about you?

We might start off our careers on the right foot because we have good mentors who guide us in the right direction, but it's up to us to find other godly counselors when our original mentors leave the picture. A few of the Jewish kings failed to do this, and their lack of responsibility directly affected their legacies. Take Joash, who ascended to the throne while still a young boy. According to 2 Chronicles 24:2, "Joash did what was right in the eyes of the Lord all the years of Jehoiada the priest." Unfortunately, this king failed to find godly counselors to replace Jehoiada. Instead, "after the death of Jehoiada, the officials of Judah came and paid homage to the king, and he listened to them. They abandoned the temple of the Lord, the God of their fathers, and worshiped Asherah poles and idols" (2 Chronicles 24:17–18).

Had Joash wanted to leave a godly legacy, he would have heeded the words of Solomon: "My son, do not forget my teaching, but keep my commands in your heart, for they will prolong your life many years and bring you prosperity" (Proverbs 3:1–2).

5. A PERSON WHO WANTS TO LEAVE A GOOD LEGACY MUST FOCUS ON LIVING LIFE TODAY.

We are called to live life today, not to dream about how history will portray us. David's epitaph, recorded in Acts 13:36, makes this clear. It reads, "For when David had served God's purpose in his own generation, he fell asleep; he was buried with his fathers and his body decayed." David served God while he was alive, and then he was gone. His legacy lives on, but the focus of scripture is on how he conducted himself while he was alive.

Not that David didn't have a reason to think about posterity. Listen to what the prophet Nathan told him in 2 Samuel 7: "The Lord declares to you that the Lord Himself will establish a house for you: When your days are over and you rest with your fathers, I will raise up your offspring to succeed you, who will come from your own body, and I will establish his kingdom. . . . Your house and your kingdom will endure forever before me; your throne will be established forever" (2 Samuel 7:11–12; 16). If there was anybody who had a right to think about how future generations would perceive him, it was David. But there's nobody in scripture who got a more final epitaph than this godly king. David lived his life in a way that ensured that he would leave a good legacy, but when his life was over, it was over.

That's what legacy is all about: the life we live now and the choices that we make today. It's not about preparing for posterity; it's about living well today. If we live well now, we'll leave behind something worth remembering.

BETTER *Than* GOLD

Few people will ever fill the position of king or CEO, but everyone has the opportunity to leave a good legacy. According to Proverbs 22:1, "a good name is more desirable than great riches; to be esteemed is better than silver or gold." We all can leave a legacy of goodness that includes a good name, a good life, a good reputation, and a good work ethic. Regardless of our station in life, we can all "let [our] light shine before men, so [that] they may see [our] good deeds and praise [our] Father in heaven" (Matthew 5:16). Our good deeds won't secure us a spot in heaven; that only comes by accepting the free gift of eternal life that is available to us through Christ's death on the cross. But if we live our life in such a way that helps others understand that there is a God who is worth seeking, we can be assured that we will leave a legacy that will endure for eternity.

And it's never too late to start building a good legacy. We may have messed up every aspect of our life so far, but today is a new day. Remember Manasseh, the evil king who led Judah astray? When God finally had enough of Manasseh's sin, He allowed the Assyrians to take him prisoner. According to 2 Chronicles 33:11, they put a hook in his nose, bound him with bronze shackles, and carted him off to Babylon. But look at what happened next: "In his distress he [Manasseh] . . . humbled himself greatly before the God of his fathers. And when he prayed to Him, the Lord was moved by his entreaty and listened to his plea; so He brought him back to Jerusalem and to his kingdom" (2 Chronicles 33:12–13).

Manasseh's conversion is a beautiful testament to God's grace. If there ever was a person who deserved to be remembered for the terrible things he had done, it was Manasseh. The Bible doesn't gloss over his wickedness, but it also shows that, through the grace of God, even the worst legacy can be rescued. Manasseh's epitaph doesn't mention his return to God, but his story shows that it's never too late to start over. No matter how badly we've handled our personal or professional life, we still have the opportunity to have a new life (and build a new legacy) as a follower of Christ.

So what do you want on your tombstone? More important, what are you going to do to make sure that your eternal epitaph records that you did what was right in the eyes of the Lord your God? The advice in Proverbs 3:3–4 is a good place to start: "Let love and faithfulness never leave you; bind them around your neck, write them on the tablet of your heart. Then you will win favor and a good name in the sight of God and man."

EVALUATING LEGACY

When your life is over, what kind of legacy will you leave? That's a sobering question, isn't it? It's a question that should not be ignored. Not only does this question concern what will remain after your life on earth is finished, but it also would enable you to gain an accurate measure of where your priorities are today. The matter of what kind of legacy you will leave behind should not be addressed on your deathbed, when it's too late to make changes. With that in mind, get alone with a good friend—or with people you trust in a small group—and take a serious, honest look at the following questions:

1. WE ALL CAN THINK OF FAMOUS PEOPLE WHO HAVE LEFT POSITIVE AND EVEN INSPIRING LEGACIES, BUT AMONG THE PEOPLE YOU'VE KNOWN PERSONALLY, WHO HAS FORGED AN ENDURING LEGACY THAT CONTINUES TO MAKE A DIFFERENCE IN PEOPLE'S LIVES YEARS AFTER HIS OR HER DEATH?

   How would you describe this legacy? What was it about this person that left a profound mark on others? Do you think this individual was consciously motivated to leave a meaningful legacy?

2. IF YOUR LIFE WERE TO END FIVE MINUTES FROM NOW, WHAT WOULD YOU LIKE TO HAVE WRITTEN ON YOUR TOMBSTONE?

   Based on how you have conducted your life—in relation to your goals, your values, and your commitments, and how you have treated those around you (your family members, your friends, your coworkers), what kind of legacy have you established to this point? Would you be satisfied if that were the final statement about your life? Explain.

3. IF YOUR ANSWERS TO THE PREVIOUS QUESTIONS INDICATE THAT YOU ARE SATISFIED WITH THE KIND OF LEGACY THAT YOU HAVE ESTABLISHED UP TO THIS POINT, WHAT DO YOU PLAN TO DO TO ENSURE THAT YOU WILL FINISH WELL—WHENEVER THAT WILL BE?

    If, however, you cringe to think about the legacy that you would be leaving if you were to die very soon, what changes would you like to make to "rewrite" your legacy? Are you willing to start implementing these changes?

PRAYING *About* LEGACY

Most of us don't like to dwell on the topic of death, but, so far, the mortality rate continues to hold at 100 percent. Ready or not, one day, your life on earth will end—in one way or another, and the final tally will be calculated. What do you think you will leave behind? What do you think your life will add up to—and what would you *like* it to add up to? Use the following prayer as a springboard for talking to God about this—sincerely and candidly.

> *God, I hate to think that after I died, all that could be said about me would be that I "passed away, to no one's regret." I would like to leave a legacy of good and be carried on in the lives of the people you brought into my life. Show me how to rearrange my goals and priorities so that I can focus on the things that really matter. May I prove to be a faithful steward in the days that remain in front of me.*

Recommended Resources on Legacy

All the Kings and Queens of the Bible, by Herbert Lockyer, Zondervan, 1961.
The Book of Eulogies, edited by Phyllis Theroux, Scribner, 1997.
First Things First: To Live, To Love, To Learn, To Leave a Legacy, by Stephen Covey, Simon & Schuster, 1994.
Legacy: A Step-by-Step Guide to Writing Personal History, by Linda Spence, Ohio University Press, 1997.
The Legacy: The Giving of Life's Great Treasures, by Barrie Sanford Greiff, Regan, 1999.

TABLE 15.1   *The Kings Remembered: Rulers of the Southern Kingdom of Judah from 930 to 586 B.C.*

Name of King	Length of Reign (age at onset of reign)	Type of Legacy	Epitaph/Legacy
Rehoboam	17 years (41)	Evil	"He did evil because he had not set his heart on seeking the Lord" (2 Chronicles 12:14).
Abijah	3 years	Evil	"He committed all the sins his father had done before him; his heart was not fully devoted to the Lord his God, as the heart of David his forefather had been" (1 Kings 15:3).
Asa	41 years	Good	"Asa did what was right in the eyes of the Lord, as his father David had done. . . . Although he did not remove the high places, Asa's heart was fully committed to the Lord all his life" (1 Kings 15:11, 14).
Jehoshophat	25 years (35)	Good	"He walked in the ways of his father Asa and did not stray from them; he did what was right in the eyes of the Lord. The high places, however, were not removed, and the people still had not set their hearts on the God of their fathers" (2 Chronicles 20:32–33).
Jehoram	8 years (32)	Evil	"He walked in the ways of the kings of Israel, as the house of Ahab had done, . for he married a daughter of Ahab. He did evil in the eyes of the Lord. . . . He passed away, to no one's regret, and was buried in the City of David, but not in the tombs of the kings" (2 Chronicles 21:6, 20b).
Ahaziah	1 year (22)	Evil	"He did evil in the eyes of the Lord, as the house of Ahab had done, for after his father's death they became his advisers, to his undoing" (2 Chronicles 22:4).

TABLE 15.1 *The Kings Remembered: Rulers of the Southern Kingdom of Judah from 930 to 586 B.C.,* Cont'd.

Name of King	Length of Reign (age at onset of reign)	Type of Legacy	Epitaph/Legacy
Athaliah (queen)	6 years	Evil	No epitaph, *per se,* but she is described as "that wicked woman" in 2 Chronicles 24:7.
Joash	40 years (7)	Good	"Joash did what was right in the eyes of the Lord all the years Jehoiada the priest instructed him. The high places, however, were not removed; the people continued to offer sacrifices and burn incense there" (2 Kings 12:2).
Amaziah	29 years (25)	Good	"He did what was right in the eyes of the Lord, but not as his father David had done. In everything he followed the example of his father Joash. The high places, however, were not removed; the people continued to offer sacrifices and burn incense there" (2 Kings 14:3–4).
Azariah (Uzziah)	52 years (16)	Good	"He did what was right in the eyes of the Lord, just as his father Amaziah had done. He sought God during the days of Zechariah, who instructed him in the fear of God. As long as he sought the Lord, God gave him success" (2 Chronicles 26:4–5).
Jotham	16 years (25)	Good	"He did what was right in the eyes of the Lord, just as his father Uzziah had done, but unlike him he did not enter the temple of the Lord. The people, however, continued their corrupt practices" (2 Chronicles 27:2).
Ahaz	16 years (20)	Evil	"Unlike David his father, he did not do what was right in the eyes of the Lord his God. He walked in the ways of the kings of Israel and even sacrificed

TABLE 15.1 *The Kings Remembered: Rulers of the Southern Kingdom of Judah from 930 to 586 B.C.,* Cont'd.

Name of King	Length of Reign (age at onset of reign)	Type of Legacy	Epitaph/Legacy
			his son in the fire, following the detestable ways of the nations the Lord had driven out before the Israelites. He offered sacrifices and burned incense at the high places, on the hilltops and under every spreading tree" (2 Kings 16:2b–4).
Hezekiah	29 years (25)	Good	"He did what was right in the eyes of the Lord, just as his father David had done. He removed the high places, smashed the sacred stones and cut down the Asherah poles. . . . Hezekiah trusted in the Lord, the God of Israel. There was no one like him among all the kings of Judah, either before him or after him. He held fast to the Lord and did not cease to follow him; he kept the commands the Lord had given Moses" (2 Kings 18:3–6).
Manasseh	55 years (12)	Evil	"He did evil in the eyes of the Lord, following the detestable practices of the nations the Lord had driven out before the Israelites" (2 Kings 21:2; 2 Chronicles 33:2).
Amon	2 years (22)	Evil	"He did evil in the eyes of the Lord, as his father Manasseh had done. He walked in all the ways of his father; he worshiped the idols his father had worshiped, and bowed down to them. He forsook the Lord, the God of his fathers, and did not walk in the way of the Lord" (2 Kings 21:20–22).
Josiah	31 years (8)	Good	"He did what was right in the eyes of the Lord and walked in all the ways of his father David, not turning aside to

TABLE 15.1 *The Kings Remembered: Rulers of the Southern Kingdom of Judah from 930 to 586 B.C.,* Cont'd.

Name of King	Length of Reign (age at onset of reign)	Type of Legacy	Epitaph/Legacy
			the right or to the left" (2 Kings 22:2; 2 Chronicles 34:2).
Jehoahaz	3 months (23)	Evil	"He did evil in the eyes of the Lord, just as his fathers had done" (2 Kings 23:32).
Jehoiakim	11 years (25)	Evil	"And he did evil in the eyes of the Lord, just as his fathers had done" (2 Kings 23:37).
Jehoiachin	3 months (18)	Evil	"He did evil in the eyes of the Lord, just as his father had done" (2 Kings 24:9).
Zedekiah	11 years (21)	Evil	"He did evil in the eyes of the Lord, just as Jehoiakim had done" (2 Kings 24:19).

The Authors

Stephen R. Graves and *Thomas G. Addington* have been business partners and friends for over a decade. For the last twelve years, they have been exploring how to blend business excellence with biblical wisdom through consulting, teaching, mentoring, and writing around the world. This mission statement, originally scratched out on a breakfast napkin early one morning twelve years ago, has been their "never lost" system as they have journeyed through a variety of entrepreneurial endeavors and experiments. They founded Cornerstone Group Consulting and the *Life@Work* journal, they speak regularly in business, ministry, and academic settings, they publish frequently, they serve on national boards, and they are active in coaching leaders toward the finish line. Both hold a doctorate, both are deeply devoted to their families, and both love the never-ending challenge of meshing real life with the message of Jesus.

About Cornerstone Group

For over twelve years, Cornerstone Group has been helping leaders and organizations navigate their way to success. We have provided assistance at every stage of the development bell curve: the exciting, confident "go go" stage; the reflective, cautious "slow go" stage; and the discouraging, confusing "no go" stage. Each stage of organizational life produces its own unique set of challenges and opportunities. Whether you are a small or large nonprofit, a family business going through transition, or a medium-sized company trying to move to the next level, we can provide a valuable helping hand. Our list of clients is impressive; our reputation is rich, and our approach is refreshing.

What We Do Best

- Identify "what's broken"
- Grow business into mass retail
- Construct a compelling future vision
- Align boards and organizations
- Coach leadership transitions
- Advise senior leaders
- Make plans happen
- Create leadership teams
- Expand into international markets

CORNERSTONE GROUP

The Art of Change

Contact us and let us send you a brochure and talk about a free White Board Session (taddington@cornerstoneco.com or (479) 236-0665/ sgraves@cornerstoneco.com or (479) 236-0664).

Index

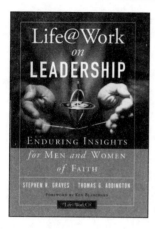

Life@Work on Leadership

Enduring Insights for Men and Women of Faith

Stephen R. Graves and Thomas G. Addington

$19.95 Hardcover

ISBN: 0-7879-6420-4

"As I struggled to find my leadership style it became apparent to me that only through a blending of faith and study could I grow as a leader. The following thoughts gathered by Steve and Tom would have accelerated my growth."
—John Tyson, chairman and CEO of Tyson Foods Inc.

"A wonderful blending of scriptural and secular insights on leadership."
—Archie W. Dunham, chairman and CEO of Conoco

What is at the heart of faithful leadership for those who lead or aspire to lead?

In one comprehensive volume, Stephen R. Graves and Thomas G. Addington—cofounders of the popular journal *Life@Work*—include contributions from the best and brightest minds currently writing on the topic of business leadership and spirituality. *Life@Work on Leadership* includes meaningful reflections on topics such as integrity, ambition, promises, roles, charisma, followership, tasks, and character.

This anthology of carefully selected readings from the very best leadership authors—John P. Kotter, Max De Pree, James M. Kouzes, Barry Z. Posner, Robert K. Greenleaf, and David A. Nadler, among others—clearly illustrates what it means to be a spiritual leader. Written with busy executives and managers in mind, each chapter examines a key word that serves as a springboard into important concepts of leadership. Each chapter also includes intriguing questions and suggestions to help you take action based on ideas in the readings.

Life@Work on Leadership will serve as a thought-provoking exploration of leadership and a much-needed blueprint for Christian leaders who want to fully integrate their faith into their work.

STEPHEN R. GRAVES and THOMAS G. ADDINGTON are the cofounders of Cornerstone Group, a consulting firm specializing in change management and strategy, and they are the cofounders of *Life@Work,* a journal that blends biblical wisdom with business excellence.

[Price subject to change]

Devotions for Leaders

Living Your Life in a 9–5 World

Harriet Crosby

$15.95 Hardcover

ISBN: 0-7879-5940-5

"What a wonderful and important tool for bridging leaders' working lives as leaders with their commitment to Christ. I'll keep a copy on my desk forever."

—Patrick Lencioni, author, *The Five Temptations of a CEO, The Five Dysfunctions of a Team,* and *The Four Obsessions of an Extraordinary Executive*

"Do not be conformed to this world, but be transformed by the renewing of your mind, so that you may discern what is the will of God-what is good and acceptable and perfect" (Romans 12:2).

Christian leaders have the spiritual resources they need to navigate the peaks and valleys of the tumultuous nine-to-five world with grace, hope, and mercy.

Devotions for Leaders is written for Christians who are leaders—or aspire to become leaders—and want to bring their spiritual lives to work. These inspiring devotions will help you discover the heart and soul of truly successful leadership through words of scripture as well as leaders who have shared their hard-won wisdom—leaders such as Max De Pree, Robert Greenleaf, Peter Drucker, James Kouzes, Barry Posner, Stephen Covey, Margaret Wheatley, James O'-Toole, and Robert Quinn. *Devotions for Leaders* gives you day-to-day encouragement to lead others with wisdom, integrity, humility, vision, energy, compassion, and faith.

Devotions for Leaders is destined to become the devotional book you rely on in whatever capacity you lead so you can be a faithful witness to biblical principles and God's love in the workplace.

HARRIET CROSBY is an inspirational writer based in Oakland, California. She earned her Master of Divinity from Fuller Theological Seminary.

[Price subject to change]

Church on Sunday, Work on Monday

The Challenge of Fusing Christian Values with Business Life

Laura Nash and Scotty McLennan

$23.95 Hardcover

ISBN: 0-7879-5698-8

How do Christians in the business world strengthen the connection between their work and their faith lives? Many believers are seeking that link but find that their churches do little to help them in their quest. In *Church on Sunday, Work on Monday*, Laura Nash and Scotty McLennan have joined forces to consider the church's need to be more in touch with business and professional people. They make concrete recommendations showing church leaders and lay businesspeople how to work in partnership to bridge the gap between pew and pulpit. This vital and much-needed book can act as a catalyst to help people at work recharge their spiritual batteries and teach them how to create constant awareness of faith, maintain a Christian life at the office, develop a true connection with their beliefs, and practice faith-based business ethics. In addition, *Church on Sunday, Work on Monday* is filled with

- Ideas for businesspeople struggling to integrate their faith lives with their lives at work
- Practical advice for transforming congregations into welcoming communities for businesspeople
- Suggestions for church leaders on how to best approach businesspeople

Church on Sunday, Work on Monday takes the popular "spirituality at work" movement into Christian territory and gives businesspeople and church leaders a framework for creating a solid alliance that will bridge these divided worlds.

LAURA NASH is senior research fellow at Harvard Business School. Prior to this position, she was visiting lecturer and program director on business and religion at the Center for the Study of Values in Public Life at Harvard Divinity School. She is the author of *Good Intentions* Aside and *Believers in Business*. In 1998 she was president of the Society of Business Ethics.

SCOTTY MCLENNAN is dean for religious life at Stanford University. He was the university chaplain at Tufts University and a senior lecturer in the area of business leadership, ethics, and religion at Harvard Business School. He is also an attorney, the author of *Finding Your Religion: When the Faith You Grew Up With Has Lost Its Meaning*.

[Price subject to change]